Chosen to Speak

A Pathway to Confident Public Speaking

Dave Arden

Albertville, Alabama, USA

Published by Warner House Press of Rimrock, Arizona, USA

Copyright © 2020 Dave Arden
Cover Design and Illustration © 2020 Ablaze Media
Interior Design © 2020 Warner House Press

All rights reserved. No part of this book may be used or reproduced in any manner whatsoever without written permission, except in the case of brief quotations in critical articles and reviews. For more information, contact

Warner House Press
1325 Lane Switch Road
Albertville, AL 35951

Published 2020
Printed in the United States of America

Unless otherwise noted, all scripture quotations are taken from the NEW AMERICAN STANDARD BIBLE®, Copyright © 1995 by The Lockman Foundation. Used by permission.

Scripture quotations marked NIV are taken from HOLY BIBLE, NEW INTERNATIONAL VERSION®. Copyright © 1973, 1978, 1984 by International Bible Society. Used by permission of Zondervan Publishing House.

Scripture quotations marked ESV are from The Holy Bible, English Standard Version®, copyright © 2001 by Crossway Bibles, a publishing ministry of Good News Publishers. Used by permission. All rights reserved.

Scripture quotations marked NKJV are from the New King James Version®. Copyright © 1982 by Thomas Nelson. Used by permission. All rights reserved.

26 25 24 23 22 3 4 5

ISBN: 978-1-951890-00-1

To Carol Lynn
(1942-2018)

Mother,
Encourager,
And sweet voice of hope

Your loving legacy lives on
In the striving for freedom
And the dreaming for a better way of life.

Contents

Chapter 1: Jambalaya Lingo	1
Chapter 2: Life in the Words	11
Chapter 3: Listening Before You Speak	23
Chapter 4: Finding your Identity	35
Chapter 5: A Coach to Champion You	47
Chapter 6: Striving for Real Freedom	59
Chapter 7: Has Your Character Been Tested?	71
Chapter 8: Speaking with the Spirit's Power	83
Chapter 9: Identifying the Falsehoods	95
Chapter 10: The Power of Sacrificial Love	107
Chapter 11: Stepping Into Your Rhythm	119
Chapter 12: Moving Forward in the Lord	129
Next Steps and Feedback	139
Appendix A	141

Acknowledgements

To the two primary speaking coaches who helped to make my transformation into a better leader possible. Thank you, Terry Witte and Don Burns.

To the churches I pastored who had to put up with
my speaking abnormalities for years, I'm grateful for your grace and support.
You are witnesses to these things.

To Steve Saccone, thank you for encouraging me to write this story
and to share this pain, and for your editorial support early in this process.

To my detractors, thanks for making the story far
better than it would have been without you.

To my wife, Rebecca, and daughters, Hope and Brooke,
your faithfulness and grace in "translating" for me
over the years has made a real impact on my life.

To Robert Warner, thank you immensely for smoothing out all the rough
places and for leaving your enduring mark here. Gadamer be blessed also;
thanks for stepping out in faith, despite the risks.

To the Chosen to Speak executive team and to the coaches
willing to serve, you are the messengers who make a movement possible.

Chapter 1: Jambalaya Lingo

People are not generally born with jumbled speaking patterns. Newborns communicate in many ways without even uttering a word. Cries for dinner and burps when full usually send a clear and true message.

But then something goes haywire.

Somewhere along the way the tongue is tied into knots of nots. As in, others are **knot** understanding. Others are **knot** on the same page. Communication is fractured and breaks down as the words do **knot** make sense.

Welcome to my jungle.

Tongue tied.

Stutterers are us…us…us.

The plane. Lands. In the water.

I don't remember how old I was when I recognized that I had a problem speaking. But over time I realized that my spoken words were not rolling out smoothly like icing on a velvet cake. Rather, my words came flying often like a haphazard pepper spray.

"Can you repeat that?"

"Pardon me?"

"Say what?"

I've heard it not once, not a hundred times, but thousands of times. On average, it's about 3 times a week. Sometimes I hear it 2 or 3 times a day.

Good first impressions are difficult to make when people struggle to understand. Relationships are weakened when there are communication gaps. Sharing and revealing our feelings is what helps us to grow in intimacy. Yet how can we communicate the innermost feelings of our hearts when we are held hostage by the tyranny of our tongue?

The Opportunity Behind the Torqued Tongue

By God's grace, however, I've learned to survive and to override these heartaches. I have developed a way to connect with people and thrive relationally as "utterly" flawed as I have been. Weaknesses are part of what it means to be human and helping people to excel past them has become The Great Opportunity to serve others and give true support.

More than just overcoming these speaking hurdles, this story is about the struggle to build character, to renovate our attitudes, to inspire vision, and to make an impact despite such flaws. More than just developing the speaker, the vision is to develop the leader who speaks.

The choice is straight-up: To maintain the status quo or to face the hurdles and work to overcome them. Stay the same or move forward.

The challenges of public speaking have been long been regarded as mankind's greatest fear. Getting in front of people to speak at a wedding, or at a gathering, or give a basic business presentation is an obstacle for many that is too high to climb.

Getting out in front of others is a test of character. Every hesitation is exposed out before the glaring eye of the listener.

Are you deterred from sharing your dreams and visions this way?

Are you allowing these snags to continue to sag your goals?

Or, are you ready for a change?

Do. Not. Stop. Reading. Now.

Lad on the Launch Pad

The problems communicating with others started in my early childhood. Multiple ear infections led to a specialist putting drainage tubes in my ears.

When the ears are infected and inflamed, sounds arrive as if one were hearing under water.

I needed speech therapy in early childhood as well. The humbling reality is that *'The Struggle'* has been a part of the story from the very beginning.

Solid speaking truly comes as the result of solid listening.

I was under water in more ways than one.

Searching upward for air.

The Rambling Youth Becomes a Rambling Man

The struggle is to mumble.

And to mumble is to stumble.

That is, the mouth is prone to garble and to ramble.

Have you mangled your words so badly that instead of "sticking the landing" (like the elegant gymnast coming off the parallel bars), the "landing" sticks you?

The origin of the word "garble" refers to a type of sieve that was used to sift spices centuries ago. The idea of "garbling" is that words are being sifted out as through a strainer/sieve so that the listener has to piece back together or to rearrange the order for the words to make sense. The word "garbling" even sounds like what it is.

Broken words lead to broken conversations.

Jumbled conversations lead to jumbled relationships.

Conversely, vivid and impactful words create the kind of word portraits that motivate, inspire, and challenge.

__Will Speak for Food__

At 24 years of age I stepped up to the platform seeking to acquire my first position as a pastor in a small church in Central Texas.

Sure, I had spoken publicly a few times at church before, but nothing quite prepared me for standing in front of a small church to speak—knowing that my future work with them somehow depended on it.

Just married two months earlier, I really needed a job to start providing for a family that I was just getting started.

Will preach for food.

Added to this, when I became nervous my rate of speech accelerated like putting gasoline to a blaze.

Step up to the platform and step into the future.

What followed next could only be called a "communi-catastrophe."

Some people speak like silk or lift their words ever so smoothly like a flute.

Not me.

I sprayed out words for 35 minutes like a cock-eyed sprinkler head spattering a sputter of spew. The pace was particularly blistering.

But there are no speed records or gold medals given in moments like these.

After I spoke that morning, the pastor search team met up with my patient wife and me and responded to us.

They. Were. Not. Impressed.

"We understood about every third word," one of the old guard said.

This is the like the golfer shanking the ball into the wrong fairway. He may eventually find the ball, **but the impact is lost.**

Nevertheless, by God's grace the church did not have a lot of options back then, so they called me as their pastor anyway.

Why would the Lord call somebody into speaking ministry who has so much trouble in this arena?

Grace. (That's for starters anyway.) Despite rattling tongues and brash fears, the good Lord gives grace over and over again.

Chosen to Speak is the reality that our calling is forged in fire.

Call it Grace with a capital G.

Undeserved favor and blessing.

Just like a good father wants to spend time with his children, so our Father likes to spend time with us.

It's still a mystery really though—Jesus, could you just find somebody else?

This moment in the spotlight is what brings our spots to light.

Keeping a positive voice matters because this **voice of ours** is what **connects us to ourselves, to others around us, and even to our God.**

Finding and **sharing our voice is part of how we find our significance and find where we fit.** Try binding the movement of a dancer with expressive body language. Try stifling the passionate lips that love to serenade a lover. Bind up the delicate fingers of the master flutist and watch those dynamic dreams diminish.

However, when we sit in the lap of a powerful Father who loves to dream, to create, nothing can slow us down.

Where we see limitations, faith sees opportunity.

"The Butt" of Being Poked Fun of

Speech problems are difficult to hide.

There's only so long you can make eye contact or show "body language" to somebody before having to actually speak.

People have responded to this over the years in a range of ways. On the lighter side, many have chosen to poke fun or even be playful. Usually, this comes in the form of a jesting, jovial type of "knock" at the speed of communication. I mean, there are some plus sides, right? For example, people are generally in a hurry to pray before they have dinner. So, it makes sense to ask the guy who speaks at the speed of sound to bless the food.

Let's dig in people.

Others have just stared at me, and I've needed my daughter to translate. In 2018, I approached the counter server taking our order at Panera Bread and simply asked, "How's-yer-day-goin?" (This came across as one word.)

The server just stared at me a minute and looked at my daughter for a reply. She had no idea what I just said. It's that blank "deer in the headlights" look.

My daughter had to translate for me.

Yet for others, this is just the type of weakness they can pounce on.

> Some have tried to fix me.
>
> Others have tried to nix me.

And somewhere after hearing even the playful barbs a hundred times this ceases to become funny anymore. Rather, it stings and at times is hurtful.

Some people have even used this weakness and insecurity to malign me, discourage me, or undermine my leadership or my influence. Oh yes, I have had people "write me off for speaking" more times than I can count.

And yet when other people write us off, I am encouraged that the story is not yet complete. By God's grace, He has given us His Word to write upon our lives. His last words about you have not yet been spoken.

A new chapter is about to be composed.

So, let's be composed.

So that we can do some composing of our own.

Follow me?

The Plot Thickens

Life became more complicated when Jesus revealed a call on my life to serve in leading and teaching a church flock.

What sense of humor does the Lord have calling someone into the speaking ministry and into teaching who really struggles to find rhythm?

To quote the leader of the Hebrews, Moses himself:

Please, Lord, I have never been eloquent, neither recently nor in time past, nor since You have spoken to Your servant; for I am slow of speech and slow of tongue. (Exodus 4:10)

In this study, we will be looking through the story of Moses' early ministry to identify the Biblical pattern of principles for renovating our communication skills.

The theme verse of ***Chosen to Speak*** is Exodus 4:11–12:

The Lord said to him, "Who has made man's mouth? Or who makes him mute or deaf, or seeing or blind? Is it not I, the Lord? Now then go, and I, even I, will be with your mouth, and teach you what you are to say."

Not Alone

Another mystery to me is why the Lord does not snap his fingers or touch my tongue and instantaneously make me a "normal talker."

Certainly that would *seem* to be the most natural approach—or at least the easiest. Yet, any radical cure bypasses the opportunity to grow in faith, in character, and in leadership.

Thank Heaven God has chosen to use others to come alongside my pathway. Integral to the main story of Moses and to my "sub-story" is the support of coaches that the Lord brings along the path to move the speaker past the lifestyle of garbling.

Two key mentors who came into my life both affirmed that it takes years to overcome speaking blockages.

"It's more difficult to change a speaking pattern than it is to quit smoking," Coach Don Burns told me.

For this writer, it was the caring people in my life (family, mentors, coaches) that God used to help me turn the corner. The Lord gave me a mother who would love me unconditionally no matter what odd form of dialect or quirky language I expressed.

He gave me a wife and children who had to work extra hard to listen to me and translate words that often get spoken with a curveball type bent.

A key elder in our Arizona startup church named Terry Witte gave me consistent feedback to sharpen my language and the message. These were the people who were instrumental in helping me to face the pains and hurts of the undercurrents. I'll share more about them later.

A local pastor allowed me to borrow his sanctuary to practice. Thanks, Andrew.

Facing the Struggle

Facing the struggle was difficult. I had heard the complaints and the criticisms for many years—even decades. If I had a quarter for every time I received barbs for speaking over the years, I could take a great vacation somewhere—overseas even.

It was easier to deny that I had any big issue.

It was easier to "kick the can" down the road.

It was easier to ignore the obvious signs.

Then. The time finally came for a true change.

These positive influencers, Don and Terry, reached out to me and offered me hope. They offered me their unconditional support; they provided what no others had previously given—the vision of a different world for me to connect deeper in speaking and relationships. Just as importantly, the Lord used them to provide the onramp and pathway to get there.

Thereafter, by God's grace, and through His Spirit, the changes gradually came. We spent several months working on slowing down the pace and interjecting more strategic pausing. More and more people responded positively.

"You don't talk as funny as you used to," a trusted friend told me in 2013.

During the two year period between 2013 and 2015 I heard more positive feedback than I had heard in the 17 years of previous teaching ministry.

The Lord used my new teaching approach to build faith and to influence others.

My only regret is that I waited so long to face this struggle.

Could God be bringing this book into your life at just the right time to help you move past your fears and insecurities? Are there people in your life right now who will lovingly listen and help give you feedback?

What's the Win?

What's the Win?

Literally, what are the best objectives to accomplish?

For starters, the Win is to overcome the speaking obstacles that can be changed and accept those speaking limitations that cannot be altered.

Discernment is vital in knowing how best to move forward. This book contains no magic, nor is this a "quick fix" to addressing the deep waters that influence speaking. However, the goal is to put you into a position to speak during a wedding or funeral. This could also be a testimony at your church. For the future business leader, the win is to give a short sales presentation with confidence. **The main objective is to get a few wins under your belt** and STEP UP with the confidence to move forward.

Along this journey, there will be some "character tests" and "leadership tests" that will come to frustrate and greatly annoy the speaker in you. In order to learn from these barriers it is imperative that the student work through these obstacles. The ultimate win is to develop and to mature past them. In following this journey, our prayer is that your leadership will deepen and grow stronger.

Another win is to develop the friends and relationships along the way that will help you grow and thrive. My prayer is that you'll connect more deeply with others and even connect deeper with God.

The Lord already knows your sputtering speaking practices. Nevertheless, He still cares about you immensely. I care greatly too. I have been there. I know how these struggles undermine confidence.

Along this pathway, another Win is to give you the vision to articulate to others how you can bring freedom to the brokenness in your own community. Walking alongside Moses—who encountered great obstacles in freeing a nation—we experience our own burden to overcome the "local bondage" in our own cities. We will go into this concept in later chapters.

What is difficult to measure right now is this: The more you expand your speaking influence, the greater the impact that is made to those lives around you. The smooth rock you throw in the wide lake will ripple out through the years.

Communication and Fulfillment

The goal of growing in communication is not merely to better connect with others, but in so doing to deepen relationships, belonging, and fulfillment.

The stronger the communication
the stronger the relationship
and the deeper the fulfillment.

For so many years I struggled for intimacy (with God and others) and therefore struggled to overcome aloneness and find the deep waters of fulfilling relationships.

There's been no greater joy and contentment than to rest in the abiding love of Christ.

Jesus put it this way:

These things I have spoken to you so that My joy may be in you, and that your joy may be made full. (John 15:11)

This love and joy comes from close relationships. And, when there are close relationships, there is potential to create meaningful and constructive life changes. That's powerful, my soon-to-be-transformed reader!

When You're Ready for a Change

Do you struggle with confidence in speaking to groups?
Have you been rambling through life without clear goals and direction?
Do you verbally or emotionally struggle to find your rhythm?
Do you struggle to live out the dreams God has called you to because of chronic limitations or communication obstacles?
Do you bury your feelings deep enough that a treasure hunter would be baffled?
Do you need more confidence in sharing the Word and your faith?
Does your community need a strong advocate and a voice for change?
If you answered yes to any of these questions, this book is for you.
Opening up our hearts to the truth about who we are inside may sound like a dangerous plan, but it is far more dangerous to ignore these signs and minimize the struggles we face.

Change can happen, by Faith. Faith changes things. His Spirit draws near.

For nothing will be impossible with God. (Luke 1:37)

The cost of maintaining the status quo is also incredibly high. Camping long term in a cone of silent isolation keeps us from being fruitful and influencing others. One day we will "wake up" ten years from now and find we have not moved an inch.

It does not always have to be this way.

I believe in you. I really **do**.

If God can take a broken voice like mine and mend it, He can surely guide you.

It's time to move ahead. This is the very day to start fresh.

Let.
This.
Be.
Just.
The.
Beginning.

Practical Notes:

Each chapter in this book will close with some coaching questions. If you want to move forward and walk through the process of strengthening skills, you will need a coach, mentor or friend to help ask key questions.

Questions for this session:

(To be shared with a coach or a friend.)
I. What positives did you find in this chapter? What challenged you?
II. What struggles have you faced in the past when speaking in public?
III. What will motivate you to push forward even when this journey gets difficult?
IV. What are the "Wins" to keep moving forward to gain confidence in speaking? (Ex: give a business presentation, speak at a wedding/funeral, strengthen your ability to teach, teach a Bible study, sing in public.)
V. What are your strengths right now as a public speaker?
VI. What weaknesses and growth opportunities do you have as a speaker?
VII. How would you define a "leader," and what dreams could you fulfill with a stronger voice?

Speaking Exercise:

What's your name and why are you interested in Chosen to Speak? Confidence assertion (speak to yourself):

"Though I struggle to be heard and to be understood, my life has purpose. I am not on this earth by accident but have been given a higher purpose. My life has value in spite of those who have criticized me or undermined me. The Hand of the Heavenly Father is not finished with me yet."

Paul puts it this way:

My message and my preaching were not in persuasive words of wisdom, but in demonstration of the Spirit and of power, so that your faith would not rest on the wisdom of men, but on the power of God. (1 Corinthians 2:3–5)

Disclaimer: What if I have learning disabilities?

Extra special attention and guidance needs to be part of preparation for anyone with learning disabilities. If you struggle to communicate basic words, extra guidance is going to be necessary. There are some difficult scenarios this book will not address.

Chapter 2: Life in the Words

Baseball Season. 1980.

The 10 year-old peewee batter trotted up to the plate. Recently "drafted" by the Oriole minions, this was his first time to bat during practice. His nerves were in overdrive.

He just wanted contact.

A hit.

Any decent hit would do.

Crack!

The skinny dark haired kid from the Northwest side of Reno hit a low roller out into left field past the shortstop.

There are few joys greater to a 70-pounder than first base. He wanted second.

He rounded the first base corner with dust blazing from his heels and zeal pumping through his heart.

Pure elation.

Raging out of the dugout the coach canceled the "celebration" mid-stride.

The "man with the fluffy mustache" crashed the play and stormed onto the field to accost the boy and reprimand him.

"#@%&!!!"

"You stupid #@&$%!!!"

"How could you do that … you $*@%$&#!!!"

The batter was now battered down.

What infraction could have warranted a public reprimand?

The hostile, bitter coach swore hard at the boy for not fading to the right after hitting first base. His mantra: No taking any extra risk. Play it safe!

The teachable moment was lost. Nobody had ever bothered to explain.

Words have the power to birth dreams or crush them before they ever get to second base. Literally.

I still remember that day from over 35 years ago.

In all honesty, I was not the greatest athlete running to base. This batter would not likely have played college ball nor made the major leagues.

Yet words leave strong impressions and deep marks. Words leave scars that endure for decades. Broken words break down worlds. The whole team heard this rant.

On the flip side, what if the coach had changed his attitude that day? What if he had celebrated that this batter was able to get a hit? What if he had publicly affirmed and supported him?

Would the future have been different? It's not likely that I would have made the major leagues, but it **is** reasonable to conclude that my attitude would have been more positive towards baseball. *Constructive words* ***do*** *create new worlds* (Genesis 1).

Our Focus in Chapter 2

In this chapter, our main character, Moses, will be introduced and we will focus on why this book has been written. More than just a book to read and put on the shelf, this guide is designed to develop your voice and to apply it to your leadership.

Speaking is an especially complex form of expression—this art form of getting the small-mighty-unwieldy tongue to dance on a dime. The writer James from the Bible compares the tongue to a small rudder that steers the big ship (James 3:4–5).

The art of impactful speaking to multiple individuals creates synergy.

Generally, public speaking does not come naturally to people. Though there are many exceptions to this, the pressure that comes from standing in front of others often unravels the one attempting to express public discourse.

How do we botch the delivery of speaking to groups or in public? Let us count the ways:

- Confusing words
- Broken rhythm
- Speaking too rapidly
- Speaking too slowly
- Too many words
- Saying the wrong word

In spite of these hurdles, the goal of influencing others is possible. Finding our positive voice helps connect us to ourselves, to others around us, and even to our God.

The Mission of Chosen to Speak is…
To help developing leaders overcome obstacles in public speaking to bring clarity and confidence to a chaotic world.

Tell Us About Yourself

Reading this book is not just about downloading information into your mind. As you read the pages, we are going to encourage you to react and to respond.

While you are reading, we encourage you to be asking yourselves questions:

"What people in my life have shaped the voice I have?"

"What words have been lifting me up?"

"What words have been pressing me down?"

The coaching questions at the end of these chapters are essential to walk through with a friend, coach, or mentor. The objective is not just to read this book but to experience this journey. The coaching element is vital to creating this experience. Speaking exercises will also help bring you out of your shell.

Moses Mumbles on the Mountain

He grew up in the powerful land of Egypt.

His voice would echo through the royal courts of the strongest nation on earth.

God would one day raise him up to rebuke the Red Sea and make waves in the nations. His words would echo down through the generations in leadership.

Yet in the beginning Moses neither sought after nor desired to speak in public.

He struggled at the outset to tame his rogue and rambling tongue.

Moses was, in our context and usage, a "Rambler."

A Rambler is (by **Chosen to Speak** definition): "Someone who sputters or utters clutter in speaking to a group. Someone who lacks confidence."

More than rambling in mere speaking, many ramble in life.

Moses is not just *any* case study in speaking. The Bible teaches that Moses was one of the most unique men to talk upon the face of the Earth.

Later this giant would become this:

Moses was very humble, more than any man who was on the face of the earth. (Numbers 12:3)

Yet the future influential icon of a man sputtered out the gate.

When called upon by Yahweh at the burning bush to go and set Israel free from bondage in Egypt, Moses pushed back and resisted with many excuses. One of these centered on his lack of speaking ability:

> "Please, Lord, I have never been eloquent, neither recently nor in time past, nor since You have spoken to Your servant; for I am slow of speech and slow of tongue." The Lord said to him, "Who has made man's mouth? Or who makes him mute or deaf, or seeing or blind? Is it not I, the Lord? Now then go, and I, even I, will be with your mouth, and teach you what you are to say." (Exodus 4:10–12)

The very man that God will one day use to carry the Ten Commandments is at a loss for words.

Moses balks, *"Are YOU talking to ME... about talking to Pharaoh? Don't you know I have a history of talking trouble?"*

The phrase "***I am not eloquent***" is literally, I am not "a man of words." Although the leader Stephen later refers to the experienced ruler Moses as a man "powerful in words and deeds" (Acts 7:22b), Moses is not confident that he can persuade much of anybody to change. Sure, he is facing a nation in slavery, but for starters he cannot move past the bondage of his own insecurities and fears.

From the linguists who study the original language, there are some major things we can draw out from this passage about his capacity to converse.

First, though Moses had received the best education in the land, he had not spoken much of the Egyptian language since he fled to Midian from Egypt 40 years earlier.

In addition, many scholars recognize there is a strong likelihood *he did have some speech impediment* given his testimony that he had carried this weakness with him for many years. Again in Exodus 6:12 (ESV), Moses refers to himself expressing remarks as with "uncircumcised lips." That is, he was very unrefined and clunky in speaking.

For certain, we know that Moses lacked confidence. He was in no mood to get into a "word shoot-out" or parlay with anybody, especially not the powerful Pharaoh.

Let This Course in Confidence Begin

Have you ever felt like Moses did? Lacking confidence and inner strength? Have you ever felt frustrated that you can't communicate what you really mean or feel inside? Have you ever known that you had serious issues with speaking out but intentionally just kicked the can down the road for years?

Building confidence is at the heart of why this book is even being written. This is a familiar experience for myself and many others.

You are not alone.

Undoubtedly for Moses those decades outside the royal courts and outside the public realm had taken a toll on his confidence. He believed himself a failure in this department and so his attitude reflected this.

For decades in my own life I refused to really face my speaking problems and the anomalies that happened when I spoke in public. There were painful feelings when it came up. I was better off not "rocking the boat" or disrupting the "status flow." And so nothing changed.

Historical Context

The story of Moses' life opens during some of the darkest days of the nation of Israel's history. The Hebrew people were suffering greatly under the oppression of the new Pharaoh who had forgotten the former ruler Joseph and his relationship with the people. This hugely powerful Pharaoh ruthlessly oppressed the peoples and heaped upon them a huge burden of affliction and pain (Exodus 1:11).

Generation after generation of Israelites waited enslaved to no avail.

Then from their great outcry the Lord heard their cries for help and responded to them by raising up new leadership. The Lord spoke to Moses at the bush saying,

I have surely seen the affliction of My people who are in Egypt, and have given heed to their cry because of their taskmasters, for I am aware of their sufferings. (Exodus 3:7)

The Lord has amazing eyesight and powerful hearing. He listens to the plight of His people, and He responds with mercy.

God's Big Plan had to be fulfilled in the right timing and He prepares the way.

Drawing Moses to a burning bush after 40 years of wilderness wanderings, the Lord unveils His plan by calling Moses to step up and to lead the people.

So I have come down to deliver them from the power of the Egyptians, and to bring them up from that land to a good and spacious land, to a land flowing with milk and honey.... Therefore, come now, and I will send you to Pharaoh, so that you may bring My people, the sons of Israel, out of Egypt. (Exodus 3:8a,10)

Wow.

After forty years of wonderings and wanderings, change is in the wind.

After forty years of obscurity, suddenly, the call to maturity.

He is truly…

Chosen
to
Speak

He is not chosen to wander through life but chosen to lead to victory.

Moses' Moment of Me, Myself, and Whine

Moses pushes back.

"Who am I?" (Exodus 3:11)

And who will I say that is sending me... *"What is his name?"* (Exodus 3:13)

Moses wonders, *"How can I take on the most powerful empire of this world?"*

Moses focused on what he could do—not what God could do through him.

His mind struggled to even imagine how God viewed him and the potential that the Heavenly Father saw in him.

His fears had him anchored to this hefty weight.

How does the Lord respond to Moses' doubts at the burning bush? Notice what he doesn't say:

He does *not* refute that Moses has a speaking issue.

He does *not* strike him down for his clear unbelief.

Rather, he says:

Who has made man's mouth? Or who makes him mute or deaf, or seeing or blind? Is it not I, the Lord? Now then go, and I, even I, will be with your mouth, and teach you what you are to say. (Exodus 4:11–12)

The Lord responds with the assurance that Moses' impediments were not an accident: **"Who made your mouth and your ears?"**

The God who made the universe created Moses Himself!

The Lord says, **"I will be with your mouth and teach you what you are to say"** (Exodus 4:12).

Here is the answer. We need to view ourselves, our world, and our circumstances as God does. We can trust His powerful Hand and true perspective to see us through.

Paraphrased from the Lord: *"Give me a chance, Moses, to use you for good and to speak through you.* **With my help, you can really do this!***"*

The Lord wants Moses to know: *"I will give you the confidence. Trust me."*

Confidence is what we're lacking. Confidence is what God gives.

With a theme of seven words, God gives a vision for the future for Israel.

The Lord says, "Let My people go" (Exodus 5:1).

In matters of public speaking, the Lord has a differing view of what the "state of our readiness" is when He deploys us into His service.

The Lord doesn't want to dredge up the murky—painful—past—history at this point, yet rather calls Moses to move forward by Faith. Thereafter, the Lord will ultimately guide Moses ahead to move past his "demons" on his journey.

How will you respond to this dramatic call?

What Excuses Do You Have?

There were other excuses. More than just identity and speaking matters, Moses had other excuses for not standing up and confronting oppression.

Moses: *"Who will I say is sending me?"*

The Lord: *"Say, 'I Am' has sent you"* (Exodus 3:14).

Moses: *"What if they don't believe me?"*

The Lord: *"I'll give you a sign"* (Exodus 4:1-5).

What are *your* reasons for not dealing with your lack of confidence in speaking?

What are the excuses that you have given for not being willing to grow in influence?

I know my own excuses which I carried for years for not addressing my speaking deficiencies.

I don't know another way to speak.
This is an embarrassing problem to bring up.
People often get used to my speaking quirks.
Change is difficult and uncomfortable.
Who can I trust to show the way?

Let's get our excuses out on the table so that we can wrestle past them. In order to change, we will need to confront the falsehoods about ourselves. To find victory, we need to move past these (self-owned) lies and not allow them to hold us back.

How Love Sees Deeper

For the "Rambler" there is great hope and encouragement in this: We can still love others and be loved deeper through the affection in our actions (1 John 3:18).

Just ask one of the biggest instigators of why this book is in print.

Her name will never make the press and she will never get to read this book on this side of heaven, yet without her, this story would surely never have been written.

Her name was Carol Lynn and she is my mother. She passed away suddenly when a brain aneurysm burst in April of 2018. Yet despite my speaking impairment, she never treated me any different. She loved unconditionally.

Carol Lynn believed that life has purpose and value and that people matter. All people matter.

Young and old. Rich and poor. Asian or Anglo or African or Indian.

She taught me how to love with a deeper love that was not just for the people who "have it all together" but rather for the people who *"need to be together."* She taught our family that we could love in more than words, but also in deeds and in caring actions.

She loved by taking meals to our elderly Mexican neighbors, Juan and Catalina.

Early on in our church life, she developed a thriving nursery ministry that cared for infants as she led out by example, cheerfully changing diapers and comforting tears.

Decades ago cloth diapers had to be washed out when they were soiled. There was no such thing as a "diaper genie." Mom was the "wiper genie" who nurtured our lives and demonstrated that we mattered to God and we mattered to her.

She was the one who encouraged me to connect to Christ.

Before coaching became a popular ministry tool, Mom was the one up in the stands at our basketball games yelling "Rebound!" for us out on the gym floor. Though she has been gone for a while now, I can still hear her voice calling us to "rebound" in life and keep moving forward.

Carol Lynn was the one to encourage me to listen to that Higher Calling from above—even though the jumbled pattern of this voice would start out rough.

She showed me *through her life* that though a voice is rugged and raw, the Father's voice still mattered and could still lift others up.

Carol Lynn demonstrated a compassion for people that never made the headlines. Yet when she passed from this life, her voice left a crater-sized hole in our hearts.

Just Make a Decision

After peppering the Lord with excuses, Moses finally rejects the Lord outright, saying: **"Please Lord now send the message by whomever you will"** (Exodus 4:13).

But the Lord, though angered at first, gives him grace by allowing his brother, Aaron, to come alongside him and fortify their position.

The narrative continues:

Then the anger of the Lord burned against Moses, and He said, "Is there not your brother Aaron the Levite? I know that he speaks fluently. And moreover, behold, he is coming out to meet you; when he sees you, he will be glad in his heart. You are to speak to him and put the words in his mouth; and I, even I, will be with your mouth and his mouth, and I will teach you what you are to do. Moreover, he shall speak for you to the people." (Exodus 4:14–16a)

How can Moses speak LIFE into the nation of Israel and liberate them with God's help when he himself is still in bondage to fear and insecurity?

Simply put, the Lord is going to give him power and guidance.

And the Lord is going to give him the words to say.

And the Lord is going to bring him a coach.

That is just like the Lord.
He is sending help to Moses...
   ...long before Moses even knows he needs help.

The Lord is not surprised by our inability to connect and to communicate with others. He recognizes that this is a real opportunity for learning and for growth.

The Lord has a large cast of coaches that he has developed for just such a reason as this. We do not have to walk this road alone.

Why This Book Was Written

This book was written to help you build confidence and know that your life has great value. Your voice has great value.

This book was written because somebody cares. With the right coaching and support, there is a pathway to overcome the stumbling blocks that paralyze us and freeze our growth.

This book was been written because your voice can be molded by the Spirit of God to lift **up** the isolated and the hurting in your community.

Like the unique prints on your fingers, you have a unique tongue and voiceprint like nobody else. Your voice needs to be heard.

Why Keep on this Journey?

Stepping onto this journey is one thing, but staying on the journey is going to take some perseverance. Why stay on the course?

First, consider the value of words and their impact on others.

Death and life are in the power of the tongue, And those who love it will eat its fruit. (Proverbs 18:21)

In spite of struggling to find our voice, we can still learn how to speak so as to encourage and build others up. Public speaking magnifies this effect.

Second, jumping on this journey will give you God's perspective and provide you peace. Good news. The Lord accepted Moses even without perfect speech so He will accept you. The Lord saw potential in Moses and He sees potential in you.

Third, how do we get past our excuses and stop undermining ourselves? *With a coach and a community of people* (who know what it is like to struggle in this arena) there is potential to get forward movement and move past our struggles.

What do you have to lose?

There's no shame in having to repeat yourself. There's nothing unique about tripping over your words. It happens to so many. There's no crime in needing support. You will surprise others with the strong benefits too!

Therefore, let's commit to grow in confidence and in the craft of communication.

Our confidence must not be merely in our talent, nor our intelligence or abilities, but in connection to our Lord who works through our limited abilities.

He declares:

My grace is sufficient for you, for my power is made perfect in weakness. (2 Corinthians 12:9, ESV)

What do you have to lose—except for your worries, insecurities and fears?

My Prayer for You

It's ironic, really. The very thing that matters most to my heart and soul is to bring meaning to a confused world.

And yet, because of my public speaking challenges, this is beyond my grasp.

Having to **truly depend upon Jesus** to help me do any of this at all, let me encourage you to consider a Heavenly Father who has no confusion whatsoever.

**My prayer is that you keep on this journey,
and discover more about yourself and
ultimately find your voice to shape our future together**.

If the Lord can use this writer (who has been kidded, criticized and critiqued), He can certainly use you too.

God is With You

Through wars and tribulation
Through fires and dark of night
When the battle seems to linger
And you can barely stand the fight.

When your world is falling in on you,
And your spirits sag so low
You can rest in these eternal words…
"God is with you wherever you go."

You may not see His joyful smile
When the dogs of doubt will bark
You may not hear his whispered voice
When the cries have drowned your heart.

But God is standing right nearby
You can nearly feel His breath.
Stand below His long shadow
And your fears face a sudden death.

When the tide turns against you
When your sorrows like rivers flow
You can always depend on one sure thing
"God is with you wherever you go."

His mighty hand to lift you up
His warm embrace you'll know.
For the Great, All-seeing, God of Peace
Is with you wherever you go.

Have I not commanded you? Be strong and courageous! Do not tremble or be dismayed, for the LORD your God is with you wherever you go. (Joshua 1:9)

Coaching Questions

I. What people in your life have shaped your voice?

II. What jumped out to you the most in this chapter?

III. What words have lifted you up and made a real positive impact?

IV. What words have torn you down and undermined your value?

V. What excuses have kept you from leading or speaking?

VI. Where have you found the value in your voice (talents, intelligence, gifts)?

VII. How can a relationship with God (or closer relationship) increase your confidence?

VIII. Who is going to be your coach (more than one is preferable)?

IX. Where has this chapter challenged you to move forward?

Speaking Exercise:

I. What excuses have you made over the years for not wanting to stand up and have a public voice?

II. Share a story from your childhood (like the chapter 2 opening) of an event which helped you to grow in character.

III. State what others value most about your life and relationships.

IV. Tell us who your favorite public speaker is and why you appreciate him or her.

Chapter 3: Listening Before You Speak

When Egypt Ruled the World

The Slave Camps in Egypt
Welcome to the City of Pain.
This is a city where mornings are met with whips.
...a city where tears run rough like rivers and aspirations are stifled by despair.
...a city where woeful parents bid their children a future of torment and their world is nurtured by nightmares.
This is a city where suffering and work seldom take a holiday–where mud and melancholy are the soup of the day...after day...after day.
A day in the life of the slave builder meant work, grunt, sweat, repeat.
Technically there was more than just one "City of Pain" in Egypt when Israel was enslaved (Exodus 1:11).
Misery loves company.

The Egyptians compelled the sons of Israel to labor rigorously; and they made their lives bitter with hard labor in mortar and bricks and at all kinds of labor in the field, all their labors which they rigorously imposed on them. (Exodus 1:13–14)

For 400 years the people of Israel had suffered oppression, hardship, and toil at the hands of the Egyptians. The rants and the chants rang out:
Where is God?
Is He really listening?
Why is He waiting so long?
What about His promise to deliver us?
The Hebrew people cried out to God again and again. Rugged, dusty, and baking, they toiled in the hot sun. They must have felt alone, broken, and forgotten.

Rebel Without a Home

When the law went forth in Egypt that every newborn Hebrew male was to be slaughtered, Moses' mother fashioned a pitch basket and sent him upriver to find deliverance through Pharaoh's daughter (Exodus 2:1–4).

Raised in the high courts of Pharaoh, Moses had access to the best upbringing and education in the land. He napped in the lap of luxury, but his heart was in turmoil knowing that his people were suffering.

Out of anger one day, Moses assaulted a guard (Exodus 2:11–14) and killed him. He was forced to flee in exile as a herder of flocks in Midian for 40 years out of sight.

He must have wondered, "Will I spend the rest of my life in mediocrity?" and "Are my best years really over?"

His future looked anything but promising.

But the Lord appeared to Moses at the burning bush and spoke, saying:

I have surely seen the affliction of My people who are in Egypt, and have given heed to their cry because of their taskmasters, for I am aware of their sufferings. So I have come down to deliver them from the power of the Egyptians. (Exodus 3:7–8a)

The Lord was listening after all.

There was hope on the new horizon.

The First Principle of Overcoming our Verbal Hurdles

Strong communication begins when listening takes priority over speaking.

This you know, my beloved brethren. But everyone must be quick to hear, slow to speak and slow to anger. (James 1:19)

The great news for the one who struggles with confidence in speaking is simply this: You can learn to be a great listener even if you struggle with the tongue.

Solomon put it this way:

Do not be hasty in word or impulsive in thought to bring up a matter in the presence of God. For God is in heaven and you are on the earth; therefore let your words be few. (Ecclesiastes 5:2)

Sounds so simple, right?

Just let others do more talking.

But, in reality, listening is one of the most difficult things to do well.

Consider Moses, our protagonist and case study, who (though a late bloomer) eventually came around to be an icon of the faith.

Moses struggled to connect with God in his early life because he really had a hard time listening and understanding. He was so focused on his own agenda that he could not really understand what God's bigger plans were for his life.

There were 3 big indicators of his real weakness in listening to God's plan and following directions. He missed out by:
- Finding his own plans for Israel's redemption
  —taking the life of the Egyptian (Exodus 2:12)

- Deliberately rejecting God's plan (initially) at the burning bush
  —inciting God to frustration and anger (Exodus 4:10,13)
- Not circumcising his son so he almost lost his life (Exodus 4:24–25)
  —His wife, Zipporah, intervened and fulfilled the requirement.

Moses' weak listening abilities were a symptom of his distant relationship with God. When we are not in tune with the Heavenly Father, we miss out on His plans, His purposes, and His encouragement.

Taking the wrong fork in the road can lead to getting a fork in the rear.

Egypt or Bust

The Lord is calling Moses to deliver His people from slavery. **Yet, three times in Exodus, Moses reminds the Lord that he has a deficiency in speaking** (Exodus 4:10, 6:12, 6:30).

"What if they don't listen to me?" asks Moses to Yahweh at the burning bush.

But behold, they will not believe me or listen to my voice, for they will say, "The Lord did not appear to you." (Exodus 4:1, ESV)

Consuming fire meets cold feet.

Moses has a difficult decision to make.

Live in the land of obscurity (Midian) and cruise into retirement, or face the past and confront Pharaoh on a road marked by uncertainty, stress, and turbulence.

The one thing that he is sure of…is that he is NOT SURE.

Confidence is far off.

He is struggling to find his purpose.

Exasperation.

The Trouble With Listening

We're not on the same wavelength.

We're not connecting.

I don't really understand.

Have you ever thought this when attempting to connect with someone?

Sound waves do travel with a "wavelength" which includes varying speeds, directions, and intensities. When we're "not on the same wavelength" then we're not in rhythm with one another and not crystalizing our thinking.

The Greek symbol for wavelength is the lambda symbol (λ).

The goal is to get on the right lambda with the Lamb (Jesus).

More important than just listening to the right wavelengths and sounds is listening to the heart and soul of a person with so many deep reflections.

Listening well is an art form and is vital in healthy relationships.

Unfortunately, early in my adult life I was a poor listener at times. I did not listen well to God; I did not understand how to listen well to my wife and I did not listen closely to other key influencers.

What barriers kept me from listening well?
>An over-confidence and self-reliance on my own abilities,
>An over-dependence on my own instincts and insights,
>A personality that often ran on overdrive,
>And a mind that struggles to slow down and process well.

Then I became stuck. Stuck in the muck.

Just when I needed it most, the long reach of God's grace stretched out to me through the hard times. The Father provided good coaches, understanding, and insightful lessons that have helped to teach me the skills and art of listening.

I believe that good listening skills are not acquired overnight but rather take time to develop. The good news is that with intentional focus and guidance, more effective listening can be accomplished.

This pathway is designed to be followed with another friend or two, or a group of people that can walk this journey together.

Are you an effective listener? Can you understand not just the sounds but the whispers, joys, fears, hurts, and cries of the heart? Does your spirit sense when others are in need or open to encouragement? Do you have the right touch with others when they are needing counsel or correction?

Benefits of Strong Listening

Why take the time to learn to become a good listener? Why seek the path of understanding?

First of all, **better listening and understanding draw us closer into intimacy in relationships** and closer toward fulfillment, longing, and peace. The failure to listen often leads to disconnection, angst, and strife. Great listeners are able to go deeper by asking meaningful questions and allowing the hearts of people to unfold before them.

Second, **strong listeners are able to discern more with better insight** into difficulties, problems, and scenarios where people are unable to move forward. Rather than attempting to merely "fix" a problem, wise listeners are able to discern heart attitudes. With the help of the Holy Spirit, they dive to the roots of the struggle, the holding patterns, the fears, the gaps, and the "life flow" blockages.

Third, strong listeners are able to carefully invest in relationships and **make a bigger impact** upon those around them.

> Listen to counsel and accept discipline,
>> That you may be wise the rest of your days. (Proverbs 19:20)

That is, listening gives us perspective that we do not gain by chatting all the time.

> *But My people did not listen to My voice,*
> *And Israel did not obey Me.*
> *So I gave them over to the stubbornness of their heart,*
> *To walk in their own devices.   (Psalm 81:11–12)*

Listening gives us security in our relationship with the Lord (Proverbs 1:33) because we are really able to come to a clear understanding of what His Will is and how to accomplish that.

When we get alone with the negative self-talk and the "voices" of isolation and fear, there is potential to build walls and to nurture our doubts. When we are too long alone with fears, we give ourselves bad advice.

When Jesus revealed His glory to Peter, James, and John, the Father spoke:

> **A bright cloud overshadowed them,**
> **and behold, a voice out of the cloud said,**
> **"This is My beloved Son, with whom I am well-pleased;**
> **listen to Him!" (Matthew 17:5)**

Getting Our Bearings

As we walk this new journey together, consider a few key proverbs in beginning.

First, consider the importance of listening without even responding:

He who restrains his words has knowledge, And he who has a cool spirit is a man of understanding. Even a fool, when he keeps silent, is considered wise; When he closes his lips, he is considered prudent. (Proverbs 17:27–28)

Fascinating.
Even the foolish man who has enough sense to keep silent is considered wise.
Sometimes the most sensible thing we can do is to keep silent.
Do you consider yourself lacking in wisdom?
Just learning to be silent at the right time can make a big difference. But it takes a lot of self-control to be shrewd enough to hold back the tongue.

Second, our tendency in listening is to hear and, while hearing, formulate our response.

Here's an idea: Wait. Until people finish speaking.

And then, formulate the response.
Lord, help me to listen. My mouth keeps getting in the way.
As the Word says:

He who gives an answer before he hears, it is folly and shame to him. (Proverbs 18:13)

For many years, I was really uncomfortable with any quiet space in a conversation.

What is it about me that when there's a quiet moment I'm so quick to fill it?

These were my own insecurities and doubts.

I was not able to feel comfortable in my own skin and just "chill."

Why?

The "flesh nature" and the "spirit nature" keep in constant battle for direction, for timing, and for control. In order to be silent, we need God's divine Spirit to provide support. If there's lots of pain in our past, our insecurities may run rampant. We need to wait upon the Lord.

So Why Doesn't God Just Heal His Speaking Outright?

Anybody who has studied the dynamic work of God and the life of Christ can see that it's not unusual for the Lord to do great wonders and to heal people of sicknesses and diseases immediately (Matthew 9:35).

So when it comes to matters of speaking correctly, why does the Lord often use a process for people to progress and improve?

Why didn't the Lord just "fix" Moses before he went to Egypt?

The Lord does what He pleases (Psalm 115:3) as sometimes the quick fix does not allow us to grow or to change. Consider how the hard times in life humble us and help us to grow in character and mature in love and faith.

Ultimately He is bringing glory to His own Namesake (Isaiah 48:9–11) and He is in the position to tell us what to do. We're not in the position to tell Him what to do.

So Who is the Lord?

Have you ever become acquainted with the Lord?

He is called "Wonderful Counselor" and "Mighty God" and "Prince of Peace" (Isaiah 9:6).

The Lord is Creator, Powerful Ruler, and Leader of His People. He does not grow tired or weary and His understanding no one can fathom (Isaiah 40:28).

He reigns over all the universe.

He is without sin and without fault in all He does (Isaiah 6:3).

He is the Everlasting One who sees and who hears the plight of broken people. He is the God who has the power to deliver from sin and suffering and carry us into a fruitful and peaceful place through Christ (John 16:33).

To know God is to have insight, understanding, and perspective that the world itself cannot give. To know the Lord is to know love, joy, and peace at the deepest levels one can imagine. To know God is to find fulfillment even in the worst of times.

Practical Help for Listening

Good listening takes practice, but here is some encouragement to get off on the right foot and the right ear.

First, after someone speaks, pause and take time to reflect on what has been said. *Are you quick to cut people off after they speak?*

Ask a direct follow-up question right after someone speaks to convey directly that you have heard them and are processing the information.

Once you've dialogued back and forth, take a moment and ask yourself: What's the main point that the other person is wanting to convey? What emotional undercurrents have caused them to express their concerns or needs?

What's the appropriate response given their predicament?

More than just repeating others' thoughts back to them, let's go deeper. We need to push more for insight.

Let's go deeper in relationships by listening to others' heart and soul language.

Are you content staying on the surface relationally?

Or do you want to go deeper?

Consider Your Local Oppression

Where is the City of Pain in your own community?

The concept of "local bondage" is described by Chosen to Speak as the "brokenness in your own backyard." Here is the equation:

Broken Character (BC) + Broken Relationships (BR) + Broken Dreams (BD)
=
Confusion and Community Chaos (CCC)

The "local bondage" in your community is more than just what you see on the surface in the frustrations—it runs deeper with conflict and fears.

Where is the aloneness than needs relationship?

Where is the discouragement that needs to be encouraged?

Where is the pain that needs comforting?

Ultimately, we're looking to identify the brokenness that might be in our own backyard. The brokenness might even be next door.

The "local bondage" in your area is the failure to reach the full potential of what God intended your community to be. The Lord created man in His image and desired man to live in completion before sin entered the world and peace was lost (Genesis 3).

Raise your level of listening.

Learning to go deeper as a listener takes time, but let's set up goals for ourselves. In conversations with others, what percentage of time do you listen? What percentage do you do the talking?

Strong listeners are going to do only 20% to 30% of the talking and 70% to 80% of the listening. Where do you stand now?

Who are the people in your life you need to be listening to more?

To what negative influencers in your life do you need to listen less?

The Decision

And so the time comes for Moses to make the critical decision:

"Do I allow my confusion and lack of faith to keep me in the same holding pattern for the future ahead, or do I throw 'caution to the wind' and boldly step forward and overcome my doubts, my fears and my past?"

Then Moses departed and returned to Jethro his father-in-law and said to him, "Please, let me go, that I may return to my brethren who are in Egypt, and see if they are still alive." And Jethro said to Moses, "Go in peace." (Exodus 4:18)

And so Moses moves forward, not knowing what the future will hold.

What about you?

Are you willing to move forward?

And…What of Faith?

How does Moses' communication story connect with our lives today? Have you ever struggled to overcome doubts that keep you from finding your voice?

You have something you want to express, don't you?

You have something you want to say, not merely with your lips, but with your life.

Something on the inside wants to come out.

A life verse cries out for meaning.

Your life is poetry,

and symphony…and song…waiting to be born.
Your message is born out of mud, and bricks…
    and torment…
    and pain.

Final Thoughts

Do you believe that God has a larger purpose for you that He can still use in spite of your weaknesses? Cut yourself some slack. You may not be ready for the professional speakers' tour, but you can still make a difference in the lives of others.

There's great news!

You can still love, still serve, and still be a really positive influence on others.

When we pray, the Lord's Spirit knows how to interpret our groans and our longings (Romans 8:26). His Spirit—also called the Counselor, Comforter, and Spirit of Life—can get to the crux of our needs and help us to find peace and find our place.

The Creator knows where we're coming from and understands our deeper needs and deeper vibes (Psalm 139).

Can you relate with this prayer? Lift up this heartbeat to the heavens.

DAVE ARDEN

The Lord is My Rock

The Lord is My Rock.
My indestructible Fort Knocks.

Limestone. Granite. Marble. Turf.
He created the bedrock of the earth.

I will not be shattered.
I WILL not break.
My rock is still beneath me
So my heart will not faint.

Boulders like birthstones are a passing whim
The big rock EARTH is just a pebble to Him.

Asphalt. Concrete. Sweet Cement.
Won't keep for eternity—nor hold your rent.
On the Lord ALONE will his people stand.
He's a MIGHTY rock—not mere shifting sand.

The Lord is my Rock I will not fear.
I'm standing for God and I will not veer
To the right or to the left, I'll hold my ground.
For Christ...the SOLID rock I've found.

The Lord my rock is a strong defense.
You can take *your* doubts and not be tense.
No cracks. No faults. He's perfect—no wrong.
His beauty and majesty are forever strong.

My feet hold firm like mountains of faith
Planted deep down—no storm can shake.

Babylon. Rome. Now the Parthenon.
Rocks of the ancients will soon be gone.

Still all of earth's granite won't keep your life steady
But the Lord's own foundation is waiting and ready.
To give your life firmness and purpose to stand
Forever He'll keep you on his treasured Land!

The Lord is my rock, my fortress and my deliverer; my God is my rock, in whom I take refuge. (Psalm 18:2, NIV)

Coaching Questions

I. What part of Moses' calling can you relate to the most?

II. What challenged you from this chapter the most?

III. On a scale of 1 to 10 (10 being greatest) how would you rate yourself as a listener? Why so?

IV. Toward which individuals do you need to improve your listening?

V. What selfish attitudes of the heart hinder your listening the most?

VI. Survey your community for healthy community:

Where is the loneliness, the discouragement, and the relational pain?

VII. Where in your community is the Broken Character (BC)?

    the Broken Relationships (BR)?

    the Broken Dreams (BD)?

VIII. Where can you make a difference in the lives of others? Pray to God that He will give you wisdom and help you with any unbelief that you struggle with.

IX. What are some practical ways to improve your listening skills?

Speaking Exercises:

I. For the benefit of listening, one of the participants share a short 3 minute speech on any topic and those listening may respond to key questions afterward.

II. Take 2 minutes and share what obstacles keep you from listening effectively.

III. Take 3 minutes and share 2 practical ways to improve your listening.

Chapter 4: Finding your Identity

Flashback: Moses is Sent up the River
   "Wait, what? You want to place our child in a basket and do what?" blasts Amram, the father of Moses.
   "Place him in the Nile, husband," replies Moses' mother Jochebed.
   "The Nile? Are you serious? Don't you know how dangerous that is? What about the crocodiles? Don't you know that Pharaoh has already been tossing Hebrew sons in the Nile to destroy them?"
   "He is a beautiful child! We have kept him for 3 months. They will kill us too if they find out we are hiding him."
   "How will he survive, mother?" continues Amram, "And, if he does survive, how will our son ever know that he belongs to us? We have suffered so much already as a people. Must we suffer still more?"
   "Let's trust the Lord. He has a plan. I'll send our daughter Miriam to keep watch by the river and see if she can keep track of him. I will offer to be a nursemaid."
   "Just rip my heart out right now, will you?"

Can you imagine a more bitter choice for any parents to make?

Keep your child and he will no doubt be killed, or set your child adrift and likely lose all connection to his future.

Moses' parents are named in the Bible from the family of Levi (Numbers 26:59). Though we don't have an exact record of their conversation, we can certainly get a portrayal of the emotional upheaval Moses' parents must have experienced.

In order to know more about the origin of Moses' identity, let's review how Jochebed, his "mother of invention," created a little cruiser made of pitch to float and to hide Moses. This basket of papyrus reeds represented a small spark of hope along the banks of the mighty Nile river.

Yet the basket was placed within floating distance of the royal bathing place and the infant Moses cried out as Pharaoh's daughter came to his side (Exodus 2:6);
   this baby brought in with the bath water.

Such is the start of Moses' unconventional life. *Even when he was living* "inside the box," he was outside the box.

These were terrible times. No longer satisfied with just making life oppressive, painful, and downright miserable for the Hebrews (Exodus 1:11–14), the powerful Pharaoh of Moses' day sought to destroy the next generation by throwing their firstborn males into the Nile River.

How difficult a challenge this predicament is, to find our voice when the future is literally adrift. Small dreams get bounced around the big winds of a turbulent world.

Do you ever find yourself in that place where your fragile aspirations are facing overwhelming odds? Have your own close family or friends harbored doubts about your future? Has your vision of tomorrow brought you to some untimely tears?

Have you ever cried out for a true compass and asked, "Who am I really made to be? What did God place me on earth to become and to do?"

How can we really find our true voice if we do not have a clear grasp of our own identity in the midst of confusing times? Let's look at how we can turn the commotion we are facing into some positive motion to excel forward.

What's your True Identity?

Identity is often defined as "the essence of being, or who a person is."

The Bible says that we are created in the "image of God" (Genesis 1:27). Specifically, mankind has been created with the capacity to reason, to make moral choices (right and wrong) and to connect relationally together. Moreover, man has been created with a "spiritual nature" and the capacity to live after death. Man is a reflection of God and the "**man**ifestation" of God's high hopes and aspirations.

Moses was trained in the courts of Egypt by the finest scholars in the land. Still, he was restless at the brutal treatment of His people in Israel. Sent into exile after killing an Egyptian who was tormenting a Hebrew slave, Moses faced an ongoing "identity crisis." See Appendix A for more on this topic.

For 40 years Moses wandered with his flocks in the land of Midian. One day he saw a burning bush blazing with fire, but the foliage was not consumed (Exodus 3:2). When he walked over to investigate the source, Moses literally heard the voice of God calling him by name: "Moses, Moses." The Lord challenged Moses to become the voice of Israel and to help set the people free of slavery. Moses was forced to confront his own insecurities, saying, *"Who am I that I should go to Pharaoh?"* (Exodus 3:11).

Moses faced further identity questions on his quest to Egypt.

He had experienced rejection from his own people (Hebrew and Egyptian both). He experienced rejection from the established government. He must have considered himself, long in exile, as rejected even by God. **We have little evidence prior to this meeting that Moses had any connection to God.**

Who was Moses, really?

A child saved from government-decreed genocide?

The son of an Egyptian princess?

A scandalous murderer?

A rogue shepherd?

A dynamic leader in the making?

The pillar on whom the nation of Israel pinned their hopes?

At one stage or another, he was each of the above. However, without a clear understanding of his own role, how could he find the confidence to stand before Pharaoh?

Moses directly questioned God, "What if they will not believe me or listen to what I say?" (Exodus 4:1).

Yahweh—Father God—responded by asking Moses a question, "What is that in your hand?" (Exodus 4:2). Moses answered by speaking of his shepherd's staff.

The Lord told him to throw it on the ground and, when Moses complied, the staff became a snake. After first jumping back, Moses was called upon to grab the snake by the tail and it became a rod again—

that they may believe that the Lord, the God of their fathers, the God of Abraham, the God of Isaac, and the God of Jacob, has appeared to you. (Exodus 4:5)

What is in your own hand that might help you fulfill your dreams? How will this aid you in your journey? Do you have a gift that will help amplify your voice?

This same staff of Moses is henceforth called "the rod of God" and will be used by Moses to help defeat Egypt. He will use it to bring forth plagues (Exodus 7:20, 8:17), open the Red Sea (Exodus 14:16), and bring forth water in the desert (Exodus 17:4–7).

Crafted by ancient tribes, the rugged sealed wood of a staff was intended to last a lifetime. The staff is a symbol of his lifelong calling as a shepherd of the flock (people) of God. Moses' authority came through his calling, and this staff would be used repeatedly as a divine tool to help guide his people and to overcome their enemies (Exodus 17:8–14).

The Lord knows your name. He is calling you to Himself.

How does your unique calling affect your voice? Not everybody is called to be a pastor or shepherd. Are you called to be a teacher? Perhaps a businessperson, doctor, or nurse? What about a craftsman or mechanic? The possibilities are unlimited.

The Lord also gave Moses another sign:

The Lord furthermore said to him, "Now put your hand into your bosom." So he put his hand into his bosom, and when he took it out, behold, his hand was leprous like snow. Then He said, "Put your hand into your bosom again." So he put his hand into his bosom again, and when he took it out of his bosom, behold, it was restored like the rest of his flesh. (Exodus 4:6–7)

In ancient times, the disease of leprosy was contagious and devastating. The afflicted, whose skin began to flake off, even endured the erosion of feeling in their nerves. These victims, then considered "unclean," were often cast out of the community. The priests were given strict guidelines to quarantine the lepers so that it would not spread to the rest of the community (Leviticus 14). They saw this bad skin as a reflection of the deeper sin and brokenness within.

How about that for a sign? Moses himself is presented with a visual reminder of his own corrupt selfish nature and still witnesses how God has the power to heal.

What about you? How can God use your brokenness (wounds) to demonstrate His power to restore?

In spite of his hurtful past and guilt, his pain and sin *ultimately* did not define Moses. He recognized over time that he was chosen of God. He was born to be an instrument of leadership and would one day deliver the nation from bondage.

Identity Factors: Relationships

Consider this: *Who am I when it comes to my relationships?*

When it comes to finding significance, our relationships have a big influence on how we view ourselves and where our worth comes from.

Have your parents helped to shape you and position you where you can find your identity and significance in the unconditional love of Christ? Or have you placed your worth in following the rules, in your performance, or the circumstances around you?

Jesus identifies himself as a Son, praying "Our Father" to Heaven above. In the gospel of John alone, Jesus refers to his relationship with the Heavenly Father over a hundred times. By faith, we can also become a close child of God.

We are clearly created in the image of God. We are created as relational beings whose purpose—in great part—is to relate to God and to relate to one another.

Jesus' greatest command in the Bible is to love God and to love one another (Matthew 22:36–38).

Have you made relationships a priority in your life? If so, how much time do you spend strengthening your relationships to make an impact on the lives of others?

Identity Factors: Character

For Moses, his character was being developed in-process. Still-not-yet the strong leader, this fledgling trailblazer was just starting to learn the identity of the "God of the Blazing Bush." Character is a part of our identity and much more difficult to give form than just words. Character is how we will be remembered now and in the future: the purity of our heart, our compassion for others, the faith of our soul, the honesty of our tongue, and the strength of our promises.

Character matters for the same reason as our backbone holds up our head, our heart, and our stomach. So it is that character affects every aspect of our lives.

As we follow God's plans, we take on His character through faith (Romans 4:1–4), by the power of His Spirit filled with love and joy and peace in Him.

Why Does Our Identity Matter?

Without a strong identity, we are prone to drifting. Have you ever questioned who you have ultimately been created to be? Specifically, what is the calling God has placed upon your life? What's your connection to the Heavenly Father? Your strengths and gifts? Your character? Your passion? What purpose and pathway lie before you?

When we don't know who we are, how difficult it is to find our voice. We start looking to others to validate our plans. When we don't know who we are, any place we live will suffice. When we don't know who we are, uncertainty and insecurity abound. When we don't know who we are, we will likely give ourselves bad advice.

On the other hand, when we do know who we are, in relationship to the Heavenly Father, we can live with peace, purpose, and direction to follow the Father's plans.

Out of this relationship, we can speak boldly, knowing that we share an eternal perspective; one which stands upon foundational principles that have stood the test of time.

The Potential In YOU

What have you been tallying to arrive at your identity, value, and worth?
The Bible teaches that the Lord finds great value in every soul.
Reflect on the following perspectives to consider the value God places on your life:

- *You were bought at a price* (1 Corinthians 6:20).

"In real estate, value is determined by what somebody is willing to pay for property," a pastor friend reminded me. "Jesus was willing to lay down His very life to acquire us and to restore us. So you are of incomparable value."

- **Behold what manner of love the Father has bestowed on us, that we should be called children of God. (1 John 3:1, NKJV)**

By His grace, mercy, and love we are bought in—by Jesus' sacrifice—and brought into relationship in the family of God.

- **Because of his great love for us, God, who is rich in mercy, made us alive with Christ even when we were dead in transgressions... And God raised us up with Christ and seated us with him in the heavenly realms ... [to] show the incomparable riches of his grace, expressed in his kindness to us in Christ Jesus. (Ephesians 2:4–7, NIV)**

The Heavenly Father is passionate about building relationships. He greatly values relationships and holds them as a treasured priority. Notice none of these passages say: "Only if you are attractive, talented, healthy and smart." Your relationship is born in the vision God has to restore humanity and to forgive—through the work of His Son Jesus.

Once we understand how the Eternal God views us (with grace, mercy, and purpose), this changes how we view ourselves. He restores us for His higher purposes to proclaim His name and expand His Kingdom.

Still, God is not keeping score like an overzealous cop. He's much more interested in the relationship and how we can align our lives to His purpose. He is more interested in our willingness to follow Him than mere behavior. He wants to go deeper with us, heart to heart. He has the power to take our self-reliant, rigid hearts and give us a heart with the sensitive spirit to love.

Moreover, I will give you a new heart and put a new spirit within you; and I will remove the heart of stone from your flesh and give you a heart of flesh. (Ezekiel 36:26)

Just like Moses' leprous hand was covered over, so our sins are covered over when we confess them to God.

Our God loves to create and loves to inspire the future. Vision and leadership are his specialty. Therefore, saying **"yes"** to God by faith is an identity game-changer. Our identity in being a child of the Heavenly Father is rooted in this: Do we even believe God exists? Are we accepting of the Father's love? Are we listening to the Father's plans? Are we willing to know and to follow His path?

Get Comfortable in Your Own Skin

Skin problems are not just a trouble of the past. I grew up in a home where my parents cared much for me, but I did not have a high regard for myself. Let's just say that I was not very comfortable "in my own skin." Of course, part of that was that "my own skin" was flawed and marred by lots of marks, potholes, and scars. During my late teens, one side of my face had not just one, but several marks that I was not proud of. When I went off to graduate school I had to take the high-powered drug Accutane.

The treatment solved one problem but created another. It caused such harsh drying that now instead of being covered with acne, my face and lips were covered in severely dehydrated skin. Years of struggling with feeling awkward took their toll on me, and, as an inevitable result, on my core identity. I understood the flesh as being weak and corrupt.

After years of struggles with my appearance and insecurities nicking away at my sense of self-worth, I was left with the realization that the ultimate problem was not in my appearance and disability. The ultimate problem was that my relationship with the Lord was weak and my faith needed more stability and strength.

Yet through these weaknesses, I was drawn into a relationship that mattered. Are you lacking confidence? What an opportunity to learn and to blossom!

Decision Time

While interacting with the Lord at the burning bush, the time finally came for Moses to make a decision:

Keep quiet and become a forgotten footnote of history, or step up and let the cry of deliverance be heard down through the ages.

We never saw Charlton Heston utter these words in the movie "The Ten Commandments", but we know they come straight from the direct story:

"Please Lord, send the message by whomever You will" (Exodus 4:13).

That is, "Lord, count me out. Send somebody else."

Have you ever had similar thoughts?

"Lord, there has to be somebody else better."

"I'm just not capable."

How does the Lord respond? Talk about getting off on the wrong bare foot with the Lord.

The Lord first gets upset, but then He encourages Moses by telling him that His coach, his own brother Aaron, is on the way (Exodus 4:14–16).

This reluctant prophet finally ran out of excuses.

Moses moved forward.

Goodbye Jethro – We're Off to Meet the Pharaoh

While wandering the lands of Midian in exile, Moses was blessed to meet a nomadic father figure named Jethro who allowed him to become part of the family and to marry his daughter Zipporah. Moses undoubtedly had mixed feelings the day he said farewell to Jethro and his large migrating clan. Jethro had been a real shepherd to Moses, taking him in and providing a place for him in his clan for 40 years.

"Go in peace," Jethro told Moses upon his departure (Exodus 4:18).

After 40 years of exile in Midian, the day finally came to leave. Packing up with his wife and sons, Moses brought the "staff of God in his hand" (Exodus 4:20). The rod of God was an ever-present reminder that God Himself had appointed Moses to lead.

This journey would be anything but peaceful.

Practically Then, How do We Find Our Identity in Christ?

First, we need to take a "God-Lens View" of ourselves.

Moses had viewed himself as an outsider. From the moment he walked into Pharaoh's daughter's life, they knew that he was a Hebrew. And yet, neither the Egyptians nor the Hebrews received him nor accepted his leadership at the outset.

But The Lord saw great potential in Moses, even in spite of his speaking problems. The Sovereign Keeper of Eternity had a plan and a purpose for Moses, to use Him for a unique role. Consider that the Lord might have a special role that He has uniquely prepared **especially for you** to fulfill.

In order to find our identity in Christ, our **relationship with Jesus needs to be a priority.** Jesus declares, "If anyone wishes to come after Me, he must deny himself, and take up his cross and follow Me" (Matthew 16:24). That is, we are invited to join him in relationship. We follow as we yield our lives and our plans to God.

The more we know about Jesus, the more we can identify with Him. By allowing Jesus' Spirit to touch our hearts, He then fills us with the fruit of His Spirit: Love, joy, peace, patience, kindness, faithfulness, self-control and more (Galatians 5:22).

We find our identity in relationship to God by pursuing the plans and purposes of God. Jesus established the example for us during his life by honoring the Father through reaching out to the sick and the hurting and teaching them the Father's ways. Jesus demonstrated the Father's plan by His willingness to serve and to sacrifice for others.

We discover our identity in relationship to God when we ultimately seek the Father's approval and not the approval of this world or its rulers.

When Jesus exemplified his life for the Father by being baptized and surrendered to do the Father's will, the voice of Heaven called out:

This is My beloved Son, in whom I am well-pleased. (Matthew 3:17)

Great news. When the God of the Universe provides His approval—through the life and work of Christ—we can experience a depth of peace and contentment that far exceeds anything this world can offer.

We can find our identity in Christ knowing that the Father is patiently molding us into the image of Jesus (2 Corinthians 5:17–19).

The Lord Himself is patient. I am amazed at how patient and gracious he has been with me; that for so many years He allowed me to "ramble" and allowed so many choppy words to bounce my voice in odd reverberations.

Yet, when I received God's acceptance and patience in relationship, He allowed me patience to find a rhythm in speaking and the opportunity to clarify my voice. In receiving His patience, we find our way back to His path.

The Lord is not slow about His promise ... but is patient toward you, not wishing for any to perish but for all to come to repentance. (2 Peter 3:9)

Rather than focusing on "Am I good enough?," we can focus on aligning our pathway to His plans. God is perfect in all His ways (Mark 10:18), so the idea that God would choose a flawed character to complete His mission speaks highly of His great grace. The path of forgiveness and mercy unfolds as Moses' journey continues.

Looking in the Mirror

Take a few minutes to look in the mirror when you speak. Watch yourself on video. Does your face, your body language, and your tone flow out of a soul that's at peace and harmony with the Father?

Identity problems create message problems. Unrest, anger, discontentment, and hurt create undercurrents that overflow in overt and subtle ways when we speak.

However, when there is joy, faith, and hope—built around our confidence in the Father's powerful plans—we can express our message with strength, knowing that there is divine affirmation to help carry the day.

DAVE ARDEN

Moses' Diary:
the Day After the Burning Bush

Am I dreaming?

What just happened yesterday at the fire?

For 40 years I've wandered with Jethro's tribe in Midian, wondering if my life would ever return to the splendor of growing up in Pharaoh's palace. Am I going back to Egypt at last?

Time to start preparing for the trip.

Who is this God that speaks out of smoke? What did he mean when he said:

I have surely seen the affliction of My people ... and have given heed to their cry.... So I have come down to deliver them from the power of the Egyptians, and to bring them up from that land to a good and spacious land. (Exodus 3:7–8)

What kind of future will this be?

I have not seen the Hebrews in a long time. They rejected me saying, "Who made you ruler and judge over us?" How will they receive me now?

Did God really just choose me? To help deliver a nation from slavery? How could he choose a guy to lead who struggles so much to speak?

How will this God carry out His plan?

And how am I ever going to face the most powerful man in the world?

What an adventure!

I'm excited.

I'm scared to death.

I'm speechless.

Coaching Questions

Identity is the intricately woven sum of our relationships, our character, our thoughts, our decisions, our faith, our intellectual/emotional health, our spiritual core, and our future. Identity is the "I" that we place in the "I love you."

I. What positives did you find in this chapter?

II. In what ways do you identify with Moses' distant relationship with God?

III. What steps can you take to guide you closer to your relationship with God?

IV. Do any identity struggles affect your ability to speak with a confident voice?

V. Trusting in God's voice, how can you push back against your insecurities?

VI. What impact does your identity have on your capacity to love God and love others?

VII. What special calling has God placed upon your life?

VIII. How much power do you give external circumstances or other people over your confidence?

IX. What's your takeaway from this chapter?

Speaking Exercises:

I. Share an example from your life when you experienced an "identity crisis."

II. Share why (according to the Bible) you are a person of worth and value.

III. Share what future dreams and aspirations you have.

Chapter 5: A Coach to Champion You

Finding Moses

Stopping at a watering hole to replenish, Aaron picked up a conversation with another traveler who asked, "Why are you making such a long trip to Midian?"

"I'm going to look for Moses," answered Aaron.

"Moses, the rogue scoundrel?" scoffed the nomad. "We haven't heard much from him for the last 40 years."

"Well, that's my brother you're talking about there. Watch your tongue! The Lord compelled me to go find him."

"Find Moses?! Why would you want to do that?"

"We need him back in Egypt," countered Aaron.

"Egypt?! Moses abandoned the region a long time ago. How could you ever trust that forgotten soul again?"

"Even if I find him all banged up, we still have hope," retorted Aaron.

"Hope? Are you kidding me? Be on your way. Good luck finding Moses."

With such a vast, lonely desert in front of him, locating Moses would not be easy for Aaron. Such a conversation begs the question: **Why not just allow Moses to wander his way back to Egypt? Why make such an effort to go in pursuit of this "lost" leader?**

In short, Moses needed a coach to instill him with confidence and encouragement. This mentor would confirm his calling.

Aaron's reputation in the Bible has long been tarnished by his antics in making a gold idol later in his life (Exodus 32), but consider the distance Aaron had to bridge in guiding Moses to his people—in both miles and in relationship (Exodus 4:14).

His unique role served a necessary and significant purpose.

Finding Moses was no small project. The questions must have been circling:

> What had really happened to Moses in the last 40 years?
> Where would Aaron find Moses?
> And what kind of person would he find when they met?

His coaching skills will be put to the test!

Muddy Beginnings

In this chapter, we will focus on why a good coach is so important to the speaking development process and provide ways to identify a new coach for your own journey.

Good coaching is vital in gaining confidence in speaking. Who will be the one to help champion your cause? Unless speaking comes naturally to you as a gift, we all need a "champion." Specifically, we need someone who is willing to go deeper with us.

Two are better than one because they have a good return for their labor. For if either of them falls, the one will lift up his companion. But woe to the one who falls when there is not another to lift him up. And if one can overpower him who is alone, two can resist him. A cord of three strands is not quickly torn apart. (Ecclesiastes 4:9–10, 12)

Isolation is not the answer. Connecting with another coach is like somebody throwing you a lifeline.

The cord of three strands is a strong hitch to tie to.

One strand is you. Another is your coach.

Who is the third strand? The Lord Himself is tied to your future.

Do you have a quality coach who can come alongside to guide you? Do you have someone you can trust to be honest about your shortcomings? Without consistent feedback from a reliable coach, how will find your way?

The Broken Record

Moses' life up to this point had been repeating itself like a broken record. The recurring theme follows this path: Rejection, pain, shame, wandering. Repeat.

If Moses life story had been a country song, he could have given Johnny Cash a run for his money. *"I struck a man in Egypt just to watch him die,"* or *"I'm rushing over to a burning bush of fire."*

Moses spent 40 years of his life roaming the hot and windy sands of the Midian desert. His feet were weathered like well-worn tires. His skin was darkened by the sun. He must have tread through many sandals searching for direction and purpose.

His shaky future rested on shifting sands. Living the lifestyle of a nomad must have been maddening. There's nothing quite so lonely as living in a land called "Uncertainty."

Brother Rescue

Meet Moses' older brother. His name is Aaron.

Aaron's leadership was a key influence in the Exodus from Egypt.

Even while Moses was "melting like butter" at the burning bush, the Lord had already sent Aaron on his way to come and meet with Moses to encourage him and help him stand up against their opposition.

Aaron greets him with an embrace and a kiss:

Now the Lord said to Aaron, "Go to meet Moses in the wilderness." So he went and met him at the mountain of God and kissed him. (Exodus 4:27)

What a comforting, encouraging reunion this must have been!

What does Aaron bring to the table?

First of all, he has clear affection for his brother. He has spent much time missing and longing for Moses' return.

Aaron cares deeply about Moses and his future. He also has the capacity to speak well.

Aaron is not only Moses' bridge to the past, but his relationship will soon become the bridge of communication and connection to the nation's future. Aaron speaks fluently (Exodus 4:16) and is able to connect with Pharaoh in his own language.

- Aaron raises the staff with Moses against Pharaoh (Exodus 7:8–25).
- Aaron becomes the first high priest of Israel.
- Fifteen times in the Old Testament, the Word says "the Lord spoke to Moses and Aaron."
- Aaron's descendants influence the priesthood for generations. John the Baptist was even a descendant of Aaron (Luke 1:5).
- When Aaron dies, the nation mourns his death for 30 days (Numbers 20:29).

Aaron helps Moses get reconnected to the nation of Israel, confront a powerful Pharaoh, and walk alongside him during critical years. Aaron is an advocate for Moses and helps champion his development.

Five Reasons a Quality Coach Makes a Difference

Let's move forward, my attentive reader.

Here are the reasons a coach is so vital:

First, we sound differently on the outside than what we hear from within. Have you ever heard yourself speak on video or audio?

That's a little scary right?

That's not me, is it?

We think we sound one way (what we hear in our head), but the reality can be quite different. And, if there has been any kind of emotional trauma early in life, the disparity is worse.

Second, we need somebody to be able to give us an honest, objective line of feedback on the effectiveness of our content and our delivery.

We need somebody with maturity who is going to speak to us in a loving way to build us up—not tear us down. We need somebody who will be honest enough to correct us when we need correction.

Third, the rates of speed, pacing, and pausing in public speaking have a big influence on how effectively the message gets through. **Coaching is critical for finding an effective rhythm and pacing pattern.**

For some of us, our tongues have a difficult time keeping up with the fast pace of our thoughts. Coaching helps throw on the brakes!

Fourth, we need to be able to monitor our progress.

The road to being more effective as a speaker is a journey filled with valleys, hills, and potholes.

To this very day, I remember little phrases that my coaches would say that would help guide me and encourage me on the pathway.

Here are some of my favorite speech "coaching quips":
- "It's more difficult to change a speech pattern than to quit smoking."
- "What's the main point and focus of your content?"
- "You talk too fast but when you quote the Bible I understand you."
- "Let's try again."
- "You need to pause more. You need to pause. Pause!"

Fifth, one of the main reasons we need a coach is that when we do fall down, we need our coach to help us bounce back and re-fortify our efforts. There are going to be times when we want to quit. We may waffle about standing up for our cause. Not everybody is going to align with us, but that's ok. Our coach will re-affirm that our voice has value and that our message is worth hearing.

Moses' Family Biz

For Moses, Aaron, Miriam (Moses' sister), and Zipporah (his wife), the "family business" was liberating the nation of Israel during the most dangerous time in their history to lead them out of slavery. The Lord speaks of them as such:

Indeed, I brought you up from the land of Egypt and ransomed you from the house of slavery, and I sent before you Moses, Aaron and Miriam. (Micah 6:4)

And the relationships Moses had with each of these were integral to his success in finding his voice and leading well. In fact, Aaron had to do most of the speaking when the two brothers first reconnected Moses with the nation and during the first meeting with Pharaoh. Later, Moses carried this speaking role by himself.

Moses had to first develop into the position as a speaker.

Let me repeat that…Moses had to develop as a speaker.

This path was a process.

This path takes time.

So then, why are we surprised when we also have to grow into the role?

Surely God is powerful enough to touch Moses and say "**Boom**" to turn him into an oratory angel overnight. But He did not choose to do so. Not to second question the Father, so let's look at *why not*.

By allowing Moses to grow into his speaking role:
- Moses would depend more upon God.
- Moses would need to seek God's vision and not his own.
- Moses would wait upon God's timing to build relationship and trust.
- Moses would have to depend upon others for help.
- Moses' character would grow more as a result of the testing.

The Lord ultimately wanted to establish His name and His reputation as the powerful God over all nations.

Discovering Your Champion

Anyone that is facing "confidence struggles" or speaking impediments needs a champion. In fact, the definition of an "impediment" is something that hinders our progress. This champion is the person that helps walk alongside us to offer support, encouragement, and feedback to overcome our hindrances. This will most likely not be one person, but rather a few people in your life who encourage you to gain your voice.

What are some qualities to look for in a "champion"?

We need someone who accepts our struggle and loves us anyway. The caring and compassion character of the coaching relationship is non-negotiable. That is, love and support are the foundation for the relationship to build upon in the future. This love and compassion is vital support to help you get through the rough patches.

Expect rough patches. Rough patches are part of the pathway.

What other qualities do we need in a coach?
- Someone who has the perseverance to help overcome obstacles.
- Someone who is patient and will be sincerely honest with you.
- Someone who is an encourager and is trustworthy.
- Someone who will caringly help you keep moving forward.

We need someone who is a good listener, who will be willing to critique our public speaking, and will also be a sounding board against which we can share our fears.

Zipporah, the Forgotten Wife, and Miriam

Women play a significant role in Moses' life story. Moses' mother certainly plays a key role because she spares him an early death. But also, consider his wife Zipporah and sister Miriam.

His wife Zipporah often receives little attention. Imagine, wives reading this, your reaction if your husband came to you one day and said: "We're moving to another country to confront one of the most powerful leaders in the world." How would you respond? Oh, and by the way, what if your husband told you that you're going to free an entire nation of weary oppressed slaves?!

Yet Zipporah's support came at a vital time.

Miriam also has a key role in praising God for deliverance at the Red Sea, leading the other women out in praise (Exodus 15:20–21).

Women have an important role in guiding, coaching, and leading. In my own case, without my mother's support, my story would not be complete. In fact, I've dedicated this book to my mother. My wife Rebecca has been a major ally of mine as well. She has helped "translate" or slow me down many times over the decades. My sweet wife has been a real "rock" for our family—loving, supportive, and steady.

We welcome mature women, young women, and even teenage girls to this journey. Our two daughters, Hope and Brooke, are being encouraged to find their voices also.

How can women play a key role in our new vision and voice?

One distinctive thing about Zipporah is that she was known to be from Cush (Numbers 12:1). That is, she was from Northeast Africa and, most likely, a woman of dark complexion. Moses and Zipporah had 2 sons together. While not the conventional choice of a wife for the time, the Lord used Zipporah to help Moses make important decisions and to provide some needed moral support.

Zipporah accepted Moses in spite of his speech impediments.

She accepted him in spite of his past crimes.

She affirmed him in spite of his being a loner and an outcast.

She received him in spite of the fact he had not found his true identity, calling, and voice.

When we're struggling to work through speech problems, we have to come to a place where we accept ourselves and where we are. *Yet more than just acceptance, we need these supportive relationships so that we can rise up and move past this struggle.*

The Word encourages us of the Heavenly Father's love:

> **As a Father has compassion on his children,**
> **so the Lord has compassion on those who fear him;**
> **for He knows how we are formed,**
> **He remembers that we are dust.**
> **The life of mortals is like grass,**
> **they flourish like a flower of the field;**
> **the wind blows over it and it is gone,**
> **and its place remembers it no more.**
> **But from everlasting to everlasting**
> **the Lord's love is with those who fear him,**
> **and his righteousness with their children's children.**
> **(Psalm 103:13–17, NIV)**

Our Heavenly Father accepts us where we are. He is filled with compassion—comforting us even when we feel at our worst.

He knows that we are dust.

The physical future of our body is a dusty one.

He keeps loving us anyway. He promises eternal life (John 3:16).

He accepts us where we are. So then we can move forward.

And He wants us to grow in relationship to Him.

The Detractors

Anybody who struggles with finding confidence in public speaking knows that not everybody listening stands up to offer support. In fact, the detractors are easier to spot.

The word "detract" is used to mean "to reduce the value or the worth of someone or something." The detractors are those who seek to reduce or de-value our worth.

Moses had detractors by the dozens and their theme was, "Who made you ruler and judge over us?" (Exodus 2:14).

For being so widely regarded as a great leader, Moses was one of the most criticized figures of all time.

Did the strong leader Moses ever get his feelings hurt?

No doubt.

Nevertheless, Moses chose not to accept their lack of vision and lack of faith for the future of the nation of Israel.

Have you ever noticed the different types of detractors that walk alongside you for a while and love to taunt along the way?

The **aggressive detractors** are the ones who don't mind coming up to you straight away and telling you that they do not like your speaking style.

"If you would just learn to slow down your speech," they gladly offer their assistance—as if you did not know that there was any such problem.

Then there are the **passive detractors** who are not as bold as to confront you to your face but they gladly deride you behind the scenes. They might even enjoy the idea of you falling down in your struggles.

The **back-handed detractors** are bold enough to make subtle undermining comments in a second hand manner that find their way back to you.

Over the long struggle to move past the pain and the nitpickers, I have come across big detractors and small detractors.

One thing all these detractors have had in common is that they really don't understand the struggle. They find that it's much easier to jump on the bandwagon of complaint, criticism, sometimes even condemnation, than hop on the bus of hope.

Detractors often outnumber those constructive advocates who work overtime in our defense. **We cannot adopt their mantra and buckle or surrender to such criticism. Their degrading tactics do not define us nor our worth.**

Getting Past the Distraction of Detraction

So how do we get past the detractors?
Keep moving forward.
Keep the vision alive of knowing that your message matters.

Consider for a moment—in your life, who are the true friends? Who are those that you can trust who would help be an advocate?

This is the time to start gathering our forces and connecting with people who can be part of the solution, rather than part of the struggle.

What about your mother, father, or siblings? Would they be willing to stand beside you and encourage you?

These relationships are vital on the road to overcoming our struggles.

What about an aunt or uncle? Your former teachers? Retired pastor friends?

Here is a short list of more ideas on where to find a potential coach:
How about discovering a caring leader at your local church?
Is there a local community leader that knows how to listen well and could be your advocate?

The Chosen to Speak network is established to help find coaches who will champion the next generation of leaders. Contact us directly to try to find someone in your area. See Next Steps at the back of this book for contact information.

During our exercises at the end of this chapter, you will start to make a list of potential coaches and narrow your search to one. In addition, there are some questions for you to "interview" your potential coach.

Does your coach have to be an effective speaker himself?

A coach does *not* have to a strong speaker. Although the prophet Aaron had the capacity to speak well, the character quality of authenticity and the skill of being a good listener are more important than speaking ability. That said, as you grow as a speaker, the ability to receive teachings from skilled orators will certainly be an excellent help.

Your coach can be that calm presence that sees the best in you and helps bring out your heart, your calling, your voice.

Their role is to help bring out the best in you, the "client." Their role is not to instill their own agenda but rather to help you find yours.

Why not look for a new coach today?

    Finding.

        A quality coach.

            Marks.

                The turning point.

                    In.

                      Your.

                          Own.

                              Dynamic.

                                Story.

DAVE ARDEN

Moses' Journeys Back to Egypt

I've traveled on the stormy sands
On a caravan called Hardship
And the winds did toss and hurl my guts
On this rugged weary long trip.

I thought, "Why the blasted misery
On this wretched painful journey?"
I wonder how this life can stand
Such an awful, raging fury.

But this crossing found me searching
For friends along the road
Who I could find some refuge in
And help me truly grow.

On this caravan called Hardship
We stopped along the trek
At Humility and Gratitude
Where Grace spared us a wreck.

Hardship wasn't so bad
When I finally came to stand
My heart's by far the stronger
From the constant, pressing sands.

Coaching Questions:

I. What excites you about having an uplifting coach?

II. What internal barriers (e.g., insecurity, pride, impatience) keep you from receiving guidance from a coach?

III. Who have been the detractors who have devalued you?

IV. Who have you been able to identify as potential coaches?

V. What are the qualities you need most in a coach?

VI. Where do you struggle the most with self-acceptance?

VII. Identify two or three possible coaches and list them here:

_____

_____

_____

Speaking Exercise:

Accepting encouragement from a coach requires humility and a teachable spirit. Describe any hurdles you have acquiring a good coach.

Here's a sample approach to finding a coach:

"**_____, I am really desiring to grow as a speaker and I need someone who I can trust to give me some constructive feedback in making a short vision/business/ministry presentation. Would you be willing to meet with me for a few months to help? I just need to ask you four questions to know if you would be a good fit.**"

Interview questions for your coach:

I. The goal is for me to gain confidence in speaking. Would you commit to helping me to grow in this area?

II. Will you be patient with me and listen well to help me move past my insecurities, fears, and speaking obstacles?

III. Would you be willing to hold our sessions in confidence?

IV. Will you commit to help me find my rhythm, even if it takes several months?

Find a good place to meet that's safe from distractions. Avoid that person who is too eager to correct or to "fix you." Rather, we're looking for someone with a relaxed coaching posture willing to come alongside.

Chapter 6: Striving for Real Freedom

Pharaoh's Agenda for Today:
Wake early to bathe in exquisite oils, sweet rich perfumes,
and the "sweat of the gods."
Lavish on the best balms in the world.
Cover up from head to toe in ornate gold jewelry,
a bold, loud necklace, and sparkling gemstones.
Breathe in your own matchless beauty.
Be dressed by servants in lush linen garments and coddle your feet.
Don't leave home without your beaded, bedazzling headdress.
Survey one of the greatest armies in the ancient world.
Tour the empire and gorge on lasting gourmet meals.
Count your wealth that the world can only envy.
Bask in your unique divine status–one of the gaudy gang of gods.
Standing before Pharaoh comes another quiet figure, Moses in contrast:
His leathered skin wrinkled by years in the desert sun.
No sweet perfume smell but rather a raw earthy aroma.
Moses' gravelly voice is shaky, shored up by Aaron.
No smooth garments or jewelry but the rugged raiment of a true shepherd.
His coarse feet battered by years of withering sands.
Not a big armory to boast but rather a band of battered slaves.
He has no wealth but abounds only in the presence and promises of God.
Moses comes with a small bark but an abundant bite. His message will echo down the centuries, simply declaring from the Lord, "Let my people go."

Moses' "Big Mo" Moment

Moses must have rehearsed the moment a hundred times in his head before he stepped in front of Pharaoh.

His tone and posture.

His faith and determination.

His courage (or lack thereof).

After all, this was one of the most powerful Pharaohs of all time. Let's set the scene. The courtroom of this majestic leader of Egypt would have been extravagant and luxurious. Pharaoh received from his regular envoys much in reverence, worship, and gifts, but he is about to get a wake-up call from an unexpected place.

Moses and Aaron came and said to Pharaoh, "Thus says the Lord, the God of Israel, 'Let My people go that they may celebrate a feast to Me in the wilderness.'" But Pharaoh said, "Who is the Lord that I should obey His voice to let Israel go? I do not know the Lord, and besides, I will not let Israel go." (Exodus 5:1–2)

Notice, Moses and Aaron both spoke together to Pharaoh. The impression is that Moses spoke and Aaron "translated" what Moses was saying. Coming before a Pharoah uninvited could be offensive in ancient times and was a major risk.

This could have cost them their lives. And Moses, at this point, is still striving to find his voice.

But wait, they were not speaking on their own authority.

A Higher Voice emboldened and empowered them.

Pharaoh responded simply, *"Who is the Lord that I should let Israel go? I do not know the Lord, and besides, I will not let Israel go."*

Overwhelming Odds

Have you ever felt this way? Stacked up against overwhelming odds? Have you been exposed as an imperfect and marred vessel in a world where *polish* is the relish of the day? This is the moment and gut check where we have to hold steadfast in the storm blast. This is one of those defining moments. Stand or run? Fight or flight?

Moses is out-gunned, out-numbered, and "out-blinged."

Still, consider this—Moses has a Great Vision for freedom.

This is freedom from oppression, boredom, scorn, and pain.

His dream is to be free of the world locked up by lucrative lockets.

Rather than being bogged down in a self-absorbed schedule every day, he is free to serve.

He is free to dream and to explore.

Free to worship and bask in God's greatness.

Free to love without fear.

Moses is free to share his vision face to face with one of the greatest tyrants of all time, with a simple call…and with the help of Aaron.

Thus says the Lord, the God of Israel, "Let My people go that they may celebrate a feast to Me in the wilderness." (Exodus 5:1)

Moses has a simple calling to start with.

His message is like a liberating light, with a simple request: "We smell freedom and we want to break free while in the wilderness to worship our God."

"You don't own us, King."

"We need some space."

"It's time that the whole community breaks free!"

Your Vision and Your Dream

The Call of God is the call to break free from a worldly system that wants to conform us to the lavish lifestyle of self-centered existence.

The worldly system oppresses the poor and the weak.

The ones with all the gold rule—that is, rule over others.

The weak suffer at the hands of the proud.

Yet in many corners of our globe, we are only one vision shy of a breakthrough. Taking a deeper survey of the scene, consider these questions:

- *Where is the brokenness in my own community?*
- *Where is the loneliness and isolation?*
- *Where is the pain?*

With a voice that echoes from the Heavens, the Lord can you use to boldly say, "Let my people go." The cry of the Lord is the cry of freedom.

Jesus' first sermon in his hometown of Nazareth cried out for freedom. He quoted from the prophet Isaiah, pulling out the scriptures that read:

> **The Spirit of the Lord is upon me,**
> **Because He anointed me**
> **To preach the gospel to the poor.**
> **He has sent me to proclaim release to the captives,**
> **And recovery of sight to the blind,**
> **To set free those who are oppressed,**
> **To proclaim the favorable year of the Lord. (Luke 4:18–19)**

And because his hometown would not accept him, they tried to kill him (Luke 4:29). Yet Jesus held in his grasp a plan to pave the wave for freedom, to grant deliverance from the dark powers of fear and oppression.

Pharaoh Pulls Out the Push Back

After all the emotional angst Moses endured in preparing to speak to Pharaoh, the moment of truth arrives and…Pharaoh was unimpressed. Not only was the monarch not receptive of the new representatives from Israel, but was angered to the point of blasting the notion of freedom out of the water from the start.

> **But the king of Egypt said to them, "Moses and Aaron, why do you draw the people away from their work? Get back to your labors!" Again Pharaoh said, "Look, the people of the land are now many, and you would have them cease from their labors!" So the same day Pharaoh commanded the taskmasters over the people and their foremen, saying, "You are no longer to give the people straw**

to make brick as previously; let them go and gather straw for themselves." (Exodus 5:4–7)

Forcing Israel to gather their own straw (which helped to hold the bricks together) was an ominous threat. The already toilsome work and quotas just became nearly impossible.

After his first dalliance with public speaking, Moses was deeply devastated (Exodus 5:22–23). He must have fallen into a deep sense of sadness and emptiness.

Wait, what? Lord, this isn't what I had in mind.
Heartache. Loss.
Welcome back, depression my "old friend."

We can imagine how broken Moses must have been that day. His worst fears were realized. His relationship with the nation of Israel was about to be tested to the core.

The news at home among the Hebrews was not well received. Literally, the foremen of Israel were in fear of their very lives. This new movement of God appears to have tripped out of the starting gate.

Talk about mud on your face–a big disgrace!

The Problems Lie Deeper

So often with long term patterns of brokenness, pain, and unresolved conflict, the problems lie much deeper below the surface.

In attempting to change life patterns and community patterns where corrupt ways have held the field for years, these *forces* are not going to go down without a *fight*.

Yet the fight we are called to move forward to is not a fight with guns and weapons. Rather this is a war of ideas fought through faith, and prayers, and love.

The problems lie deeper within the human heart.

To quote the old adage: "We have met the enemy and he is us."

The Bible says:
- No one is righteous, not one (Psalm 14:3).
- Man's heart is deceitful and corrupt (Jeremiah 17:9).
- All have sinned and fallen short of God's glory (Romans 3:23).

And sadly, freedom from captivity comes with a high cost.

Jesus put it simply, **"Whoever sins is a slave to sin"** (John 8:34, NIV). That is, self-centeredness and self-reliance place us in bondage to self-absorbed thinking and selfish living.

Sin and pride and lust drive us to serving ourselves above serving God and others.

How can we move past the oppression and control of power and fear?

Restoration must take place. The Bible teaches, **"Without the shedding of blood, there is no forgiveness"** (Hebrews 9:22). The Lord required the sacrifice of an unblemished lamb to cover the cost of sin. Mercy and grace, come down to the front.

Moses has a secret weapon against the land of Egypt that will one day be unveiled. The sacrifice of the lamb is a reflection of Jesus Christ Himself, the Lamb who takes away the sins of the world (John 1:29).

Another deeper problem is that others hold power over us by the opinions they hold on us. In many cases, the power they hold is not a physical threat or bondage like the leader of Egypt held, but rather an emotional bondage or "stronghold" over us. They have limited our opportunities for growth or advancement. They try to define us or narrow our vision for the future.

Consider the outcome of letting people that hold "power" over us to **keep** that power. Often this keeps us in the same pattern of living for years…even decades…or longer. Who has been keeping a "power grip" on your future?

This is a choice we make to let them have that power over us.

We can choose differently.

We can choose by Faith to place our identity in relationship to our God.

The apostle Paul puts it this way: **"It is for freedom that Christ has set us free"** (Galatians 5:1, NIV).

How do we define "freedom"? Freedom is not just the absence of pain and bondage. Freedom is pursuit of God by walking in abundant faith, love, relationships, and service so that we can move forward to become complete and established in Christ. Freedom—more simply put—is moving from "stuck" to "unstuck."

Opposing Forces

Moses and the people of Israel are stuck. They are stuck in a holding pattern they need deliverance from.

In the great "tug of war" of moving forward, often it helps to list out those "forces" that are working for us and those "forces" that are working against us.

The List of things Working Against Moses:
- His reputation as an unknown outsider
- Deep skepticism about his leadership
- Speech and confidence problems
- Inexperience in leading a nation
- An extremely powerful nation that stands against him
- He is without an army, without a budget, and without any weapons

The List of Things Working For Moses
- He is reluctant, but willing to follow God
- He has a nation longing for hope
- A faithful God who can use anybody or anything
- A powerful God who knows how to overcome darkness
- Key leaders (like Aaron and Miriam) stand with him

Moses needs a miracle, and by God's grace he is going to receive a series of them. If we are stuck in a holding pattern, how can we possibly move forward? From a coaching perspective, we either have to add to those forces pushing forward or we can decrease the forces pushing against us.

Who and what are those advocates that stand with you?

Who and what are those blocks that stand in your way?

Let's trust the Lord who made your mouth to give you the vision to speak. The battle is won by **faith** and by **prayer** as the Lord listens to the cries of the people and overcomes by the Power of His Spirit.

The arm of the Lord is not too short to save, nor his ear too dull to hear. (Isaiah 59:1, NIV)

The battle to deliver our communities is not a short one.

Rather, we are entering into a long and protracted war.

A Broken Rhythm Uncovered

That morning in mid-June 2003 had started off well enough. Things were looking up. I had been interviewing the month prior in the San Jose area in consideration of planting a new church. After a few years working through growing pains with the church we helped get started in Irving, Texas, I was ready for new doors of opportunity to open. I had set my "helicopter-tractor" sprinkler on that morning to go full throttle on our thick grass.

My dreams were at full throttle too, I thought.

When I went out to pick up the heavy cast-iron sprinkler, I bent over and...

Torque!

Ouch!

The pain ran for miles.

I had thrown my back out. Hobbling back into the house, I knew my day was over. Stick a fork in me, I'm done. Back then, a "thrown back" meant I was down for two or three days recovering.

Fortunately—or so I thought—I had some muscle relaxers at the time and decided to take them. Then things went from bad to worse. Since I hadn't eaten that day, the muscle relaxers soon became harsh on my empty stomach.

I was standing in the bathroom, and then my 6'4"and 250 pound frame collapsed beneath me.

I grabbed the shower curtain as I passed out on the fast lane to the floor. By God's grace, my wife Rebecca was there at the time and helped cushion my fall, or I would have hit my head.

So, there I lay, with my underwear at my knees, my wife frantically calling 911 and my world heading to unconscious uncertainty. Fortunately, I woke up in time to tell her to pull up my pants before the paramedics arrived.

Something was definitely wrong. We just did not know what.

My life was out of rhythm, literally.

When the Sirens Finally Fell Silent

When we finally arrived at the hospital emergency room, this season of uneasiness went into full swing. For the next four days I stayed at the hospital where they discovered a half-dollar-sized hole in my heart's atrial wall. While I had been born with this gap, I never knew about it until age 34.

The body's "life blood" normally receives oxygen from the lungs and flows from your lungs back to the heart and out to the rest of the body. With this defect, much of the blood returns to the lungs—taxing the lungs and my heart. This had enlarged my heart and put me on a much faster pace to the grave.

"You are at high risk for a stroke," the doctor told me. Suddenly, I was wondering if I was going to see my young daughters grow up.

I had been bound by a heart condition that I did not know even existed. My heart had been pumping...pumping...pumping in overdrive and had been so out of rhythm that this was leading me down the pathway of desperation.

Lying in the hospital room, I cried out to the Lord for peace, and deliverance, and restoration.

How ironic to find myself in bondage to struggles that I did not even realize existed below the surface.

Giving Yourself Permission

Have you ever taken a moment to pause and consider that you have pain in your life that you have never dealt with? For many, the tendency is to bury our emotional pain so deeply that not even an archaeologist can find it.

Have you kept your pain hidden?

Have you cried out to God for help and wondered if He has heard you?

Often this nagging pain is easy to ignore. Or, perhaps we are inclined to deny the pain. Or we numb it out through a host of coping mechanisms.

We have to give ourselves permission to admit that this pain is real.

We give ourselves the green light and courage to face the pain.

For years I had been moving down life's pathway not even realizing that there was not just a physical issue below the surface, but also that I had been stuffing some emotional pain below as well.

And, more than just giving permission, we need to acknowledge that, by faith, God is big enough to handle and deal with this pain.

Do we have enough faith to consider that God can comfort and restore us in spite of this pain? Our attitude will so affect our altitude and how far we climb.

Heart Finally in Sync

On September 11, 2003, the time finally came to face the music. On the table at UT Southwestern Medical Campus in Dallas, a heart specialist placed the implant (non-invasively) up my artery and into my heart so that they could close this big gap.

I was literally awake on the table when the first attempt was made and I could feel them working inside my heart.

The. Most. Surreal. Moment. In my life.

My lips were quivering when they put the implant in my heart. The wire was tugging at my chest. "Are you sure I should be awake for this?"

Finally, they were able to place the implant into the heart and plug the gap.

Like somebody throwing a switch, suddenly my body started to feel warmer.

Wow!!! Is that how you're supposed to really feel?

I never knew.

Thank. You. Jesus.

Though it took a few months for the heart to establish the new normal, by God's grace I was able to push forward and to carry on.

The Lord Himself specializes in battered hearts. Not only does he help us work through physical issues, but the emotional ones as well. "Closing the gap in my heart wall" has become a metaphor for how he healed my hurts and closed the gap in my relationship with Him. Getting into this new life rhythm literally gave me the opportunity to start with a new heartbeat.

Where's the Break in Your Rhythm?

In light of Moses' quest for freedom for His people, where is the gap in the rhythm of your life story? What "tug of war" struggles keep you from finding freedom? What's holding you back from discovering the peace and strength to move forward by faith?

Facing the past and confronting the "forces" (internal and external) that are bogging you down is vital to being able to get to the roots of our fears and insecurities.

In this session, during our coaching time, we will identify where the bondage is and locate those positive "forces" that will give us the traction we need to press on.

Where Do You Need Freedom the Most?

In order to speak with confidence, where do you need to experience freedom the most?

- Freedom from the sin and selfishness that undermine your voice?
- Freedom from the power that others hold over you?
- Freedom from the emotional pain that holds you down?
- Freedom from the past?

Although we cannot control how other people respond to our message, the great news is that, by God's grace, we can hold firm to our message and focus on those things that we can influence.

Jesus said, **"In this world you will have trouble. But take heart! I have overcome the world"** (John 16:33, NIV).

We *can* stand on our faith, knowing the call of God is upon our life and message.

We *can* keep an upbeat attitude and focus on what we are thankful for.

We *can* prepare to the best of our ability for the day we speak, trusting in God's greater vision and power to overcome.

Still, in order to overcome, we must face the pain and doubt. Confront the bondage by identifying those tethers and ropes that want to hold us back.

This is a test of faith in our broken communities. Do we believe things are going to always stay the same? Or do we really believe God has the power to break the bondage of sin, self-reliance, oppression and doubt?

Thankfully, the story isn't finished yet.

Moses pours his heart out to God. Tomorrow is a new day.

My Heart Must be Crying Real Tears Tonight

Moses' Journal Entry When Pharaoh Crushes His Dream

My heart must be crying real tears tonight
I'm losing my sense of what's wrong and what's right.
The salt from my sorrow and the hurt in my heart
Is keeping my soul all alone in the dark.

Lord, I believed that you'd stay by my side
But where have you gone that you like to hide?
Have you quit on me now and left me alone?
I knock on your door—feels like nobody's home.

My heart must be crying real tears tonight
I don't know if I'll get up and walk to the light.
Each time I fall down and get up once more
It takes so much longer to get off the floor.

My heart must be crying real tears tonight,
But I can't *just give up* and quit this old fight.
My flesh may be weary, my soul may be hurt
But God you're my refuge and you value my worth.

My heart may be breaking and my spirit rusts
But God please renew me—in You I will trust.
My steps may falter as the storm winds blow
But the Lord is my shepherd—Your voice I still know.

Coaching Questions:

I. Where did you identify with Moses the most in this chapter?

II. Where have self-centeredness and sin made you a slave?

III. Who in your life "holds the power" over how you view yourself?

IV. What forces have held you back from moving forward?
(For example, friends, family, systems, attitudes)
List them here:

_____

_____

_____

V. What forces are helping you push forward?
(For example, doubts, detractors, faith, systems, attitudes)
List them here:

_____

_____

_____

VI. Where are the pains from your past and relational gaps that undermine your message? Where can you find comfort to heal from your past?

VII. How will God's greater vision guide you forward?

Speaking Exercises:

Tell us about your sector of the community:

I. Share where you are seeing the brokenness, aloneness, and pain.

II. Share a testimony or story (out loud) to others of where you've seen God working (either in your life or the life of a friend).

III. Who are the comforters in your life that ease the pain? Describe them.

Start praying about how God would use your testimony to bring freedom to your home and to your community. Start praying about how your voice can transform lives around you. Start praying for what Words of God to say.

Chapter 7: Has Your Character Been Tested?

Five workers toil in the hot sun.

"First, we have to mix the topsoil and the water," one of Israel's foremen bellows out. "Next, we're going to add the straw." *He pauses.*

"Well, we're a little short on straw. Ever since Moses riled the master, we're now having to gather our own straw, so we have less to work with."

"Bricks with less straw?!" one of the workers laments.

"How can we make the quota of bricks with less straw?" pops another.

"Quit blabbing and get to work!" yells out a crusty Egyptian taskmaster.

"And then we mix the mud with our feet for four days," continues the foreman, "The bricks dry for a few days; we mix some more, and pour it into the brick molds."

Crack! The sound of the thick whip upon the back of the foreman echoes down the valley. One thin drop of blood oozes slowly off the man's dry, scarred back and drips onto the sand.

"Then we'll let the bricks dry for a week," continues the foreman.

"Curse Moses who put us into this position," one of the workers whispers to another, "He had to open his big mouth. Aaron too!"

"When will this torment ever end?" The foreman thinks to himself.

The harsh new work orders from the top affected hundreds of thousands of slaves. The responsibility for this back-breaking burden fell squarely upon the shoulders of Moses and Aaron.

The crack of the lone whip echoes down the banks of the Nile River; five lonely spines sink low.

The Threats, the Frets, and the Sweats

Events for Moses were now moving from bad to worse. Not only was his message rejected and the workforce of Israel forced to gather their own straw, but the labor situation was becoming even more perilous.

> **Then the foremen of the sons of Israel came and cried out to Pharaoh, saying, "Why do you deal this way with your servants? There is no straw given to your servants, yet they keep saying to us, 'Make bricks!' And behold, your servants are being beaten; but it is the fault of your own people." But he said, "You are lazy, very lazy; therefore you say, 'Let us go and sacrifice to the Lord.' So go now and work; for you will be given no straw, yet you must deliver the quota of bricks." (Exodus 5:15–18)**

Instead of crying out to God, the leaders went to Pharaoh. He criticized the labor leadership, calling them "lazy" and unwilling to work.

The outcome is that these foremen were being beaten and in fear for their lives.

The key leaders that only weeks before had whole-heartedly embraced Moses and the Vision of Freedom suddenly became distraught.

When they left Pharaoh's presence, they met Moses and Aaron as they were waiting for them. They said to them, "May the Lord look upon you and judge you, for you have made us odious in Pharaoh's sight and in the sight of his servants, to put a sword in their hand to kill us." (Exodus 5:20–21)

Literally, the nation of Israel had become an obnoxious smell to Pharaoh. Once compliant servants, they stood now as adversaries.

They were even starting to smell like death. So Moses cried out to God:

Oh Lord, why have You brought harm to this people? (Exodus 5:22)

Has your own voice ever been tested by circumstances that are bigger than you and outside your control?

Has your voice been welded by faith, peppered with resolve, and shored up by the fortitude to ride out the storms that come when your vision of freedom breaks forth?

In this chapter, we face the reality that developing strength in our voice comes from having true character, perseverance, and rugged determination in difficult times.

The context of the struggle also has a bearing on the leader's voice. *Consider this important principle rising from Paul's letter to the Romans:*

Not only so, but we also glory in our sufferings, because we know that suffering produces perseverance; perseverance, character; and character, hope. And hope does not put us to shame, because God's love has been poured out into our hearts through the Holy Spirit, who has been given to us. (Romans 5:3–5, NIV)

The apostle Paul is encouraging the seeking believer to "glorify" or to "commemorate" his sufferings—his trials and troubles—for the benefit of growing in character, endurance, and hope.

The Biblical Principle is this: God's Character, Plan, and Promises are bigger than our speaking faults, obstacles, and bitter circumstances. His Spirit will prevail through them.

In order for metal to be forged well, the elements must endure both intense heat and pressure. By faith, character is also forged by enduring the trials and troubles of hard times.

Love and perseverance are tested when all else seems to be failing and falling down around us. Paul continues to affirm how the Spirit of Christ responds to faith and empowers us in such times to stand firm in the midst of great tests. The Spirit of Christ is a comforter and a gift.

There's a relationship between character and confidence. The greater the capacity to withstand adversity, the more enduring the voice.

We can't lose sight of the vision.

Are you ready to press forward through the obstacle course of trials?

Are you going to face the challenge or retreat in silence? When you get knocked down, can you get back up and keep standing?

When the Bottom Falls Out, the Lord Responds

The Lord responds to Moses' outcry and tribulations in a fascinating way. Notice how the Lord does NOT respond:
- He doesn't say, "Just relax Moses, everything is going to be alright."
- He doesn't say, "Everything happens for a reason."
- He doesn't say, "Wow, let me show you my 'shocked face.'"

Rather, the Lord responds with His identity and His character:

I am the Lord, and I appeared to Abraham, Isaac, and Jacob, as God Almighty,... Furthermore I have heard the groaning of the sons of Israel, because the Egyptians are holding them in bondage, and I have remembered My covenant. Say, therefore, to the sons of Israel, "I am the Lord, and I will bring you out from under the burdens of the Egyptians, and I will deliver you from their bondage." (Exodus 6:2a, 5–6a)

How does the Lord respond? He affirms the authority of His Name.
In the Bible, God's name is a reference to His unshakeable character.
He is the Lord. He is above all kings.
He is above all powers and forces of the world.
Moreover, He has a **Big Plan** and Lasting Promises for the nation of Israel. This **Big Plan** He established with Abraham many years earlier.
The Lord also has compassion for them, hears their cries, and will deliver them.
He will even give them a new land with a future:

I will bring you to the land which I swore to give to Abraham, Isaac, and Jacob, and I will give it to you for a possession; I am the Lord. (Exodus 6:8)

Sometimes there are going to be many who stand in opposition to the Big Plan of God. They don't share the vision of freedom and peace. Look at the contrast in language between Pharaoh (Exodus 5) and the True Lord Himself (Exodus 6):

Pharaoh	*The Lord Himself*
Who is the Lord?	*I am the Lord.*
I will not let Israel go.	*I have established my covenant with them.*
Why are you distracting them?	*I have heard the groaning of the Sons of Israel.*
Get back to your labors!	*I will bring you out from the burdens of Egypt and deliver you.*
No more straw for you.	*I will redeem you. I will take you for my people.*
You will not rest. You are lazy, very lazy.	*And I will be your God. I will take you to the land.*

Do you see the difference?

The King of Egypt wanted to oppress the nation of Israel and keep them in bondage, but the Lord wanted to bless the people and free them to worship and to serve. The King of Egypt wanted to harass and blast the people to get the most labor he could get out of them. The Lord wanted to adopt them and empower them by His own hand and His own peace.

Often times our world system is not trying to build us up, but rather the powers that be strive to tear us down.

The words of discouragement sting.

Rejection brings despair.

Time to Dig Deep

Such is the time to dig deep, my Rambler companion.
    For such days as these are when character walks the high wire.
Do not look down at the perilous ground below,
    Nor look at your trembling knees.
Rather, look to the solid ground and the platform out front.
    Keep your balance on the big shoulders on which you rest.
The Lord carries you on His shoulders.
    Your confidence rests in God's Character and your Calling.
Though your tongue is tangled at times,

The coarse texture of your message will draw others to hear.
Though your voice may quiver and even whimper,
The outcry of the oppressed will still be heard.
The message of freedom echoes onward.
The vision of independence resounds through the ages.

Where are Your Gaps?

Are there any character gaps in your heart, life, or soul? Are there relational gaps where you are disconnected with God and with others? Are there gaps because of emotional pains or deep fears that have never been resolved? Where does it hurt, really?

How do we know that faith is real and sincere without testing?

The times of testing are refining.

The times of testing are renewing.

Destabilization is an opportunity to stabilize stronger in the Lord.

In order to close the gaps, we need to have a healthy self-diagnosis.

- Where is the lack of faith?
- Where is the shortage of courage?
- Where is the shortage of determination?

The fleshy part of us (the Bible calls it the "old nature") is very predictable. This "fleshy mushy" nature is self-seeking, impatient, wanting attention, and sometimes "melts like butter."

Yet, by faith, the Lord empowers those who hear His voice and call upon His name. His arm is not too short to save, nor is his ear to dull to hear (Isaiah 59:1).

Good character can be contagious and so can bad character. Have we surrounded ourselves with individuals who are critical all the time?

Do not be deceived: "Bad company corrupts good morals." (1 Corinthians 15:33)

More than just identifying the gaps in our character, we need the strength and power of Jesus to fill the gaps and fortify our faith. The vision is to thrive by building a strong community.

As Moses' story unfolds, we come to realize that not only does the speaker have to persevere to overcome difficult times, but often, nearby people do as well.

Consider the story of my own coach Don Burns. Notice his predicament and how the circumstances and context affected his approach.

Coach Don Burns' Story

Back in 2012, my wife and I were seeking God's leading in finding a solid church. We had heard about a new church that was meeting in a local elementary school and felt led to pay them a visit. When we arrived, we saw numerous old friends that we had met along the way.

We found some chairs and settled in. All went well until the pastor (whom we had never met before) stepped up and started to preach. At least, I think it was preaching, but it could have been an auction almost as easily. The pastor was talking so fast that I thought there must be a fire scheduled and he needed to get done before it started! At the end of the service, I was worn out from trying to keep up with him. I was able to catch a few tidbits from his sermon and from what I could make out, it seemed that he was at least trying to present God's message for these people.

Everyone there seemed to be taking it in stride so I was left wondering what was wrong with me that I had gotten so little from the sermon. Later that afternoon, I asked our friends what they thought of the sermon and it came out in the conversation that they liked the pastor a lot and prayed for him regularly but admitted that he was a bit hard to follow and they needed to listen pretty "fast" or they would get left in the dust. They did say that with time they were able to get a little more from his sermons than the first time they had heard him as they got used to how rapidly he spoke, but that it was still pretty difficult.

In visiting with Pastor Arden after the services and before we moved on, it was apparent that his "preaching" voice was the same as his conversation voice and I soon found myself avoiding him, as I had such a hard time understanding what he was saying. I kept quiet as we settled in nicely to the new church that we had found, but I couldn't stop thinking about how much of the work and prayer that Pastor Arden was putting into preparing for his sermons was ineffective. I asked myself, "Do you think that Dave knows how fast he speaks and that people are not understanding him?" Likely so, I thought.

"So why doesn't he slow down?" I wondered. No answer for that one. Many months went by and I just couldn't get that "auctioneer" out of my head. Somebody needs to tell him to slow down. More months went by. Who am I to tell a pastor that he is a lousy public speaker?

God told me, "Dave Arden puts his pants on one leg at a time just like you do." I knew that I owed this pastor my honesty even if he had heard it before. I got Dave's phone number, but was too nervous to call, so I sent him an email instead.

Though I was nervous, it was very much to my relief that Dave was truly humble enough to know he had a speaking problem (thanks to his wife and a few others) and he knew he needed to change but did not know how.

Dave and I and the pastor at the church that my wife and I were then attending made a commitment to each other to do what we could to coach Dave and to be brutally honest with him, but that honesty would be mixed generously with brotherly love.

The three of us met regularly and Dave would "practice" his sermon presentation on us. I held a loud noise maker in my hand, and whenever the "auctioneer" began to creep in, there was a very annoying, loud interruption from me and we would talk about what was happening and he would have to "rewind" and try it again. Ever so slowly, Pastor Arden began to see the value of long pauses and speaking with single words rather than "one word paragraphs"!

Reality Really Bites

Ouch. Thanks, Don, for sharing your story. For nine years our church (River Church in Cottonwood, Arizona) had to bear up under my "rapid fire" turbo teachings every week. We even had two sweet greeters, Ron and Joyce Smith, who encouraged newcomers to give the "auctioneer" a chance. "He's a good pastor and you get used to it," they said.

The people of the church loved me and loved my family, accepting me with speaking flaws and all. The elders affirmed our leadership and showed us grace, giving constructive feedback that I could use to sharpen the message and find my speaking voice.

This story would not have been written without them.

Thank you Terry & Janine, Ed & Kathy, Kent & Lou, Jeff & Maria, Steve & Carol, and Doug & Barb, who were our faithful elders and their wives. And thank you, gentle flock, for giving me the opportunity to serve and to shepherd while learning how to find a rhythm teaching. In addition, Pastor Andrew Puett hosted our first Ministry meeting at a church in a neighboring town. We needed a safe place to regroup.

Five Character Gauges

After Moses received encouragement from the Lord, he strove to encourage the nation. However, the "sons of Israel" still did not listen to Moses or lift their attitude on account of their cruel oppression (Exodus 6:9). For the third time, Moses recounted his own inadequacies in public speaking (Exodus 6:12).

Character is the capacity to stand up under pressure and heat that would otherwise cause us to melt like butter. Experiencing stress is a part of being human, but how do you endure in the fire?

Here are five quick gauges of character:

#1: Fight or Flight—When the stress and anxiety come, will you face the challenge in front of you or will you run for cover and flee the scene?

This is not the time to run like a mouse but rather to roar like a lion.

In the life of the leader David, this young boy faced a monstrous gladiator named Goliath who stood over nine and a half feet tall (1 Samuel 17:4). Yet the boy David did not shrink back, but withstood the test with character.

Are you willing to keep focused long enough to advance your cause?

#2: Own Your Mistakes—and learn from them. So often the temptation is to blame others for our mistakes or character shortcomings. Taking responsibility means identifying that we still have areas to learn and to grow.

He who conceals his transgressions will not prosper, but he who confesses and forsakes them will find compassion. (Proverbs 28:13)

Owning your mistakes means acknowledging how the outcome of those decisions has impacted others in a negative way. For example: "Because I cussed at you, and you responded with pain, this put distance in our relationship."

#3: Responding To Criticism and Rejection with Grace—When you are under fire with verbal scorn and ridicule, how do you respond?

The one who is quick to respond and retaliate invites trouble.

A gentle answer turns away wrath, but a harsh word stirs up anger. (Proverbs 15:1)

The one who is patient, responding with grace, deflects an explosive situation.

While anger is a natural human response and emotion, the Word says, "Do not sin in your anger" (Ephesians 4:26). The more filled with Christ's presence (through His Spirit) the more patient we become.

#4: Crazed by Delays?—When you face delays and detours on the path to your dreams, do you want to quit and give up? Or do you patiently bide your time and endure waiting until you can keep moving forward?

Let perseverance finish its work so that you may be mature and complete, not lacking anything. (James 1:4, NIV)

Do we survive delays and patiently endure them?

Or do we throw in the towel?

The believer who begins to identify with Christ receives the persevering Spirit of Christ which helps hold up during the test. Far more than just "willpower," the Holy Spirit gives peace and strength.

#5: Self-Centered or Servant? - Another gauge of character is our willingness to make others a priority over our own wants, desires and needs.

Jesus demonstrated character by putting others before Himself, not only saying, "The good shepherd lays down his life for the sheep" (John 10:11), but also demonstrating His love by laying His life down to serve and to forgive others.

The Testing of Our Character

How do we measure character? How do we rate endurance? Is it based upon any particular scale of units, weights, or degrees? Ultimately, character has to be tested by the intensity of hard times, the weight of harsh challenges, and built up in and through the fire. The Lord says:

Behold, I have refined you, but not as silver; I have tested you in the furnace of affliction. (Isaiah 48:10)

Like metal is refined in the smelter, the more your character is tested and torched and refined, the more your voice gets polished and honed.

The power of your message is not built on the mere number of words, but the capacity of faith and love (1 Peter 1:3–9) that amplifies its power and hope.

For instance, Jesus spoke of his own character saying,

I am the resurrection and the life; he who believes in me will live even if he dies. (John 11:25)

His message is amplified a hundred times by His life story and testimony of overcoming great suffering, death and despair.

One of the biggest encouragements in working through gaps in public speaking is the idea that our lives will speak much louder than mere words.

Where are the Gaps, Really?

Be honest with yourself. Where are the hidden character gaps that you may not see? What holes in your integrity are most likely to undermine your message?

Which vices threaten our effectiveness the most?

What effects do pride, jealousy, rudeness, anger, ingratitude, or imbalance have on our voice?

What is your greatest threat from within?

Let's be honest with ourselves by owning these and striving to work past them.

Do. Not stay. Where you are.

Push forward.

DAVE ARDEN

For the Cause

Five Field Workers Rambling Out Together in Song

Troubled days. Lonely nights.
We're so ready to quit the fight.
Leaders falling make us pause.
Is the way of faith just a lost cause?

Still I'll stand for the Cause of Life.
Though my back is battered by surly stripes.
I don't know how—for the road is steep
But I can't quit now—lest the Cause retreat.

The nation's at risk. Strange new laws.
They make us wonder about our deepest flaws.
Are we a people who are faithful and true?
Will we sell our soul for the devil's due?

Yes, we'll stand for the Cause of Life.
Dig for the courage to walk upright.
Guide us, O Lord, to higher ground.
We'll stay the course and receive the crown.

We must fight for the Cause of Life.
'Til our deathbed calls us to say good night.
The Cause, the Cause must be held up high.
Give your heart so the Cause won't die.

Coaching Questions:

I. What positives did you find in this chapter? What challenged you?

II. As a developing leader, what future threats on the horizon are testing your faith and your character?
(Your "where's my straw for the bricks" moments).

III. Which part of your character is tested the most when you speak?

    Faith   Self-Confidence   Nerves   Insecurities

IV. Of the five character tests, which one do you struggle with the most?

- Fight or Flight
- Owning Your Mistakes
- Responding to Criticism and Rejection with Grace
- Crazed by Delays
- Self-Centeredness or Service

V. How are you going to overcome the current character tests that you're going through?

Speaking Exercises:

I. Share about a character test you are experiencing in working to bring freedom to your community.

II. Share about a time you received criticism for your ideas or work and how you responded.

III. Share how the name of God has a powerful impact on your life and future.

Closing Note: It's hard to change a flat tire when you are in bumper-to-bumper traffic, or you are driving 40 mph down the highway. If you are facing life struggles, it's time to get off the road and find out where the leak is coming from. Talk to your coach.

Chapter 8: Speaking with the Spirit's Power

When Fear Walks Into the Room
"You really think you can win, Moses?"

"Who are you? What are you doing here?"

"Fear here.
Just have to ask,
Why would Pharaoh ever listen to *you*?"

"You are such a tormentor of souls."

"Seriously, though, why return
to the place that banished you?"

"*Why not?*"

"How are you going to help Israel
escape when you cannot
even escape your own insecurities?"

"Haven't you heard?
I'm assigned to rattle Pharaoh's cage."

"Have you seen Egypt's powerful military?
They will crush you like a fly."

"There are definitely flies in Egypt's future,
but don't you know that mighty homes are
destroyed by a multitude of small bugs?"

"If people really knew who you were,
they would never follow you, Moses."

"Here you go again. Panic. Panic. Panic.
That's the only song you know how to sing."

"Moses, you will surely die in the
wilderness just as you lived."

"I would rather live in the wilderness with hope
than in hell with you."

Here Comes the Clash

Have you ever been intimidated by threats, fears, or authorities who want to stifle your hopes and squelch your dreams?

If you could communicate with your fears face to face, what would you say to them? How many big fears would be in the room?

The *modus operandi* (MO) of fear is to intimidate and harass us. Fear comes into our midst bold and loud, really just wanting to tear us down. Our fears love to feed on themselves and celebrate when our aspirations have become ashes.

The good news, though, is that fear does not have to have the last word.

Fear is part of our natural human response and can be confronted as we discover how empty its threats really are when compared to the grace, power, and authority of the God of the Universe.

Every person that has walked the face of the earth has dealt with fears. Many have succumbed to their "spread of dread." However, when our fears are isolated, confronted, and stripped of their power, they run off "naked" into the forest.

What fears have been attacking you the most lately?
- Fear of failure?
- Fear of rejection?
- Fear of pain?
- Fear of the unknown?

Fears are big on "talking," but short on "walking" with any kind of clear conviction and understanding. They offer no leadership, with the exception of leading us away from relationship and commitment.

Drill down and get to the core of what unsettles your soul.

Don't let your faith or love falter.

Keep Pushing Forward and Still Forward

Surrounded by low morale, deep resentment, and constant criticism, Moses has few options. Trust God or retreat. Hunker down for the battle or hide out with Fear.

Just when It looks like the roof is going to fall in, the Lord ups the ante.

The Lord speaks again:

But I will harden Pharaoh's heart that I may multiply My signs and My wonders in the land of Egypt. When Pharaoh does not listen to you, then I will lay My hand on Egypt and bring out My hosts, My people the sons of Israel, from the land of Egypt by great judgments. The Egyptians shall know that I am the Lord, when I stretch out My hand

on Egypt and bring out the sons of Israel from their midst. (Exodus 7:3–5)

The Lord is planning to multiply His powerful deeds and trample on oppression with his armies or "hosts." Yet, His purpose in showing His strength is not just to throw His weight around randomly to tread upon His opponents.

Rather, the Lord wants to exalt His Name and reputation to solve the mystery: *Will the Real God please stand up!*

Literally, His message is:

The Egyptians shall know that I am the Lord. (Exodus 7:5)

This is a battle of forceful wills, and yet the winner is the one that can prevail by more than mere words or excellence of speech, but rather by the Power of the Spirit and the Authority of the Eternal God.

The question as we get deeper into the story becomes not,

"Who can shout the loudest?"

or

"Who can sound the most eloquent?"

Rather, the ultimate question is: *"Who has the power to exercise the highest authority and who will prevail in the end?"*

The apostle Paul puts this Biblical principle in place in his own life and ministry when connecting with the church in Corinth. He says:

And when I came to you, brethren, I did not come with superiority of speech or of wisdom, proclaiming to you the testimony of God. For I determined to know nothing among you except Jesus Christ [and His sacrifice].... And my message and my preaching were not in persuasive words of wisdom, but in demonstration of the Spirit and of power, so that your faith would not rest on the wisdom of men, but on the power of God. (1 Corinthians 2:1–5)

That is, Paul's goal is not perfect eloquence, speaking with a "zero margin of error," but rather to lift up Christ (and His redemptive sacrifice) and to make His kingdom known. This happens as God's supernatural presence arrives and empowers man to know that He is real and that His power and love are authentic.

Surrounded by Snakes

The Lord compels Moses and Aaron to speak to the court in Egypt with language they can certainly understand. More than just turning a rod into a serpent as he had done for Israel's leaders earlier (Exodus 4), the Lord compels them to send a louder message.

Moses and Aaron return to the court of Pharaoh and, when asked for a miracle, Aaron throws his staff down and it becomes a "serpent" (Exodus 7:10). This time, a different word [*tannin* in Hebrew] is used to describe the new creature, more likely translated as "dragon," "large serpent," or "crocodile."

Central to the lifestyle of the ancient Egyptian was the imagery and understanding of the Nile River. The Nile flooded every year and provided abundant irrigation for the lush farmlands along the river that would feed multitudes.

Symbols from the River Nile like the crocodile and the hippo were worshipped in god-like status and reverence. The crocodile was even a symbol of Egypt and their power.

What happens next is raw, bizarre, disturbing and like something one might see in a Sci-Fi movie. Pharaoh calls upon his magicians to repeat the miracle. And this is exactly what these sorcerers do (Exodus 7:11).

Powers of evil and darkness can perform miracles too.

Even at the end of times, the anti-Christ will win the masses by miracles and alleged powers (2 Thessalonians 2:9–10).

Yet Aaron and Moses prevailed as...

Aaron's staff swallowed up their staffs. *(Exodus 7:12b)*

The larger, stronger dragon devoured all of the other serpents.

This *striking* image of Aaron's work to swallow up the adversary shows how the Lord overpowers and even consumes His enemies. Famous London pastor Charles Spurgeon had a field day with this[1].

Snake-bit.

Viper sniper.

Reptiles—it's what's for dinner.

Just when you thought Moses was going to take another one on the chin, God sends a message through his servants of victory over defeat.

Aaron and Moses are not going to be intimidated. Aaron is out front this time.

The fight is on.

At this point on our journey, we zero in on just what exactly it is that's standing in our way of freedom and progress—strongholds holding us back. With the Lord's help, we can identify the obstacles and barriers to our progress.

And we can defeat them.

---

[1] Spurgeon, C. H. (1863). The Power of Aaron's Rod. In The Metropolitan Tabernacle Pulpit Sermons (Vol. 9, pp. 409–420). London: Passmore & Alabaster.

The Bite Bigger than the Bark

We throw around a common phrase in English when somebody talks a bigger talk than their actions. That is, we say, "his bark is bigger than his bite."

In this case, the dragon bite of Aaron and Moses is bigger than the bark of Pharaoh's henchmen:

> **But now, thus says the Lord, your Creator, O Jacob,**
> **And He who formed you, O Israel,**
> **"Do not fear, for I have redeemed you;**
> **I have called you by name; you are Mine!**
> **When you pass through the waters, I will be with you;**
> **And through the rivers, they will not overflow you.**
> **When you walk through the fire, you will not be scorched,**
> **Nor will the flame burn you. For I am the Lord your God,**
> **The Holy One of Israel, your Savior." (Isaiah 43:1–3a)**

Praise God. He has the power to overcome our obstacles and give us the confidence and ability to overcome the rivers and currents that come against us from all sides.

How does the Eternal power of God swallow up earthly powers?

First of all, Our Lord has the *Time and Perseverance* to overcome. Man's words and promises fade over time, but God's values and promises and Words last eternally beyond time. Jesus declares:

> *Heaven and earth will pass away,*
> *but my words will never pass away.* **(Matthew 24:35, NIV)**

Next, Jesus has the sheer *Strength to reign with power* over all those forces that would try to undermine Him.

He knows that the Power of Truth and Righteousness prevails (Psalm 89:14).

The Lord has authority over nature, over all kings, and even over all demons.

No enemies can withstand His majesty, glory, and power.

Third, The Lord has great *Depth and Understanding*.

We see life from one angle at a time usually, but our Lord God sees it all.

Nothing in all creation is hidden from God's sight. Everything is uncovered and laid bare before the eyes of him to whom we must give account. (Hebrews 4:13, NIV)

Human wisdom takes into account the human perspective, but divine wisdom takes on the divine perspective. The writer James contrasts the wisdom that is earthly (envy, selfish ambition) with the wisdom that is divine (pure, peaceable, mercy-giving, impartial, sincere) (James 3:14–17).

So then, how do we affirm others with the "right word at the right time"? The Spirit of Christ speaks through us. The love and grace of Christ drives out fears and helps us to work through all of our insecurities (1 John 4:18).

Growing Past Our Fears

The good news is that you have chosen a pathway and a test that is going to require you to look deeper inside yourself, and also to look to the bigger world and context around you.

What a great opportunity to grow! Let's look inside ourselves and look to God for help as we learn to trust in Him.

We can ask:
- Where does my confidence reside, really?
- How will I be comfortable in circumstances outside my control?
- Does my voice and message align with God's character?
- Is my message more powerful than my fears?

Not only does our deeper relationship with God help us to overcome our fears, but so does the deeper relationship with our community.

The Stroke Has Struck

In the Fall of 2005, an influential businessman joined our fledgling church plant in Cottonwood, Arizona, with his loving wife Bobbie. Persevering Ray had spent a career developing land and new communities, primarily in Phoenix. He even shared a dream of helping the church to someday build a new sanctuary.

Then, in the Spring of 2006, tragedy struck. Ray had a devastating stroke.

The doctors told him, "You'll never walk again. You'll never talk."

His wife Bobbie rallied to his support. The church came alongside as well.

At 79 years of age, Ray had already seen his vibrant years pass by him. How was he going to "bounce back" after already living nearly eight decades of life?

Despite the struggle and the long odds, Ray started working to get stronger.

"No quit," Ray's mantra was soon established.

Fighting through the fears, the brain blockage, and the struggle to take one step, Ray started into rehab.

Just walking across the room became the mountain to climb.

To push for one step. Then push again.

First three steps.

    Five steps.

        Then ten.

Just speaking a whole sentence meant going into overtime.

To utter three words.
    Five words.
        Then ten.

One step at a time, Ray learned to walk again.

And Ray learned to communicate.

Over and over again, the people in the church family and community cheered him on.

Though confined largely to a wheelchair and needing support to accomplish basic tasks, his dream of getting around and speaking became a reality.

Though he struggled with physical pain, sadness, and loneliness—feeling at times a hostage to his own body—he pursued a deeper relationship with God and did not give up on his dream to make a difference in the community where he lived. Though his sentences sometimes sputtered and didn't come to full completion, he started to communicate his faith, and his love for others.

Though it took seven years, Ray finally realized his dream by seeing the church built and completed. He walked down the main aisle of the church during the opening services.

At this writing (in 2019), he still lives at age 92 and still has a heart to see people come to know the love of Jesus.

Your voice and your message do not mature in isolation.

As you speak, your message flows out of your culture and context.

Practically Moving Past Our Fears

Specifically, how do we overcome the fear of stepping out? Let us do some diagnostics to discern where the sources of our fears lay buried.

Some of our fears are rooted in emptiness and isolation. Aloneness holds us in check. We do not have the relationships and the affirmation and encouragement of God and others. When we are left surrounded by our own negative voices, we "give ourselves bad advice."

Some of our fears are rooted in our past hurts. That is, because others have criticized us or maligned us, there is a brokenness of heart that holds us back from really standing up for ourselves. We exercise dubious plans based upon our "emotional reasoning": Since we feel deeply inadequate to cope with life challenges, then we really must be inadequate. Emotional health is certainly a real part of our make-up, but we cannot simply walk by emotions. We must walk by faith, purpose, and hope.

Some of our fears are rooted in unbelief. We fail to believe deep down in ourselves that we have value. We fail to believe that our lives have purpose. We fail to believe that we are uniquely created with a Divine blueprint. And we fail to believe in the Power and Presence of God Himself.

And some of our fears are rooted in the nature of being human. That is, we are fleshy-mushy people who are vulnerable to obstacles and opposition. Our flesh loves to "melt down like butter" and go into "Barney Fife mode" when tough times come. So, we need to know what triggers the flesh and then how to respond.

If we just keep listing all of our fears here, good listener, then we will bog ourselves down. And so the SUM of all our fears is what keeps us from really moving forward and accomplishing all that God intends for us.

Remember, Aaron's staff (dragon) ate *all* of the other serpents—not just a few!

Push back Against Fears

Rather than surrendering to our fears, let's fight them.

Fears *enjoy* getting into our face and pushing us down. So we need to push back!

The way to push back is to stand firm on the true statements that affirm our value, our faith, and our determination to stand behind our voice.

We have to verbalize—internally or externally—the importance of our message.

Remember how greatly valued you are. Remember the unfathomable love and grace by which God chooses you. Remember how faith and love put fear on its heels.

Moses wrestled internally to find the authority to speak with power.

The Heavenly Father encouraged him at the bush.

"'I Am' is sending you."

Moses had a "higher authority." The Word of God expresses that authority.

The Lord puts it this way:

> **I am the Lord;**
> **that is my name;**
> **I will not yield my glory to another,**
> **or my praise to idols. (Isaiah 42:8, NIV)**

While it may feel at times like you are a "lone voice in the wilderness," the Heavenly Father is ready to guide, to encourage, and to affirm His purpose prevails.

Who on Earth is the Holy Spirit?

The Lord has not given us a spirit of fear, but another kind of spirit.

Jesus called Him the "Helper" or the "Advocate" (John 15:26).

He comes and goes like the wind (John 3:8).

He draws us into a relationship with Christ and reveals who Jesus really is.

Who is He? He is the Holy Spirit.
- The Spirit speaks the words of God (John 3:34a).
- He speaks many languages and is without any limit (John 3:34b).
- He is called the Spirit of Truth (John 15:26) and He is filled with Life (John 6:63).

His main role is to testify to the greatness of Christ (John 15:26–27). **The Spirit helps to connect us to God and to one another by discerning hearts and motives.**

When the Holy Spirit arrives boldly, so does the presence of God.

The Holy Spirit nudges us and "convicts" us of sin (John 16:8–12). That is, we are convinced by His presence and understand the burden of our wrongs.

Over the years I am more and more amazed at how the Spirit empowers our faith and gives courage in even the darkest of times. Jesus calls Him "He" so we can relate to Him as part of the Godhead. The Spirit enlarges our abilities to connect with one another and guides us to deeper levels of communication.

The Holy Spirit is literally an inexhaustible "tool box" of "helps." Yet He has a distinct personality so that we can connect with Him uniquely.

Praise God that, even when we are not hitting all words on all cylinders, the Spirit of God can hit home with others as His strong impressions impact them, showing that the power and love of Christ is **real** and **true**.

The Spirit of Christ empowers character growth and the increase of wisdom and understanding. The Spirit of Christ connects us to true friends that help encourage us on life's bumpy trek.

When we build our lives, we build with duct tape.

But when the Spirit builds lives, He builds with Eternal Power and Purpose.

Without the Word of God and the Spirit of God, relationships are just duct-taped together and they don't last. However, with the Spirit of God we can stand firm and keep standing.

Jesus says that the Spirit works in our "weakness" (2 Corinthians 12:9).

That is, when our flesh is crumbles, His Spirit rumbles deep into our lives to shore up our insecurities and provide us with His power.

How Does the Spirit of Christ Affect Our Voice?

When our message is aligned with the Spirit of Christ:
- God is glorified.
- The peace of Christ fills hearts with love, joy, and deep rest.
- The Holy Spirit transforms lives.
- Wrongs are confessed.
- Faith and character become mature.

In effect, we see real results as people make God's agenda a priority.

War of Words

Without the Spirit of Christ, words are often used to start wars, family fights, community brawls, or even altercations between nations.

How will your words alter the world in which you live?

Will your message inspire hope or incite division?

How will your voice build others up, and not tear them down?

Conversely, words can be used to reconcile: To restore marriages, to cast off guilt, to open the doors of forgiveness, and to bring comfort and peace.

Craft your message with care.

Aaron let the Power of God—through the staff—do the talking.

In Pharaoh's response, not even the destruction of his magicians' snakes changed his heart to let Israel go (Exodus 7:13).

Aaron Confers With God

I'm groaning for your coming Lord
and my heart is going to bust.
I'm grasping for some relevance
before I turn to dust.

I've seen your hand at work up close
where snakes have come so near.
I'm searching for your better way
to overcome my fear.

I'm groaning for deliverance
and freedom from the pain.
I'm looking for some mercy
to block out all the strain.

I'm groaning for a country
that's ruled with righteous hand.
I'm yearning for security
on God's own chosen Land.

Oh Lord please come and visit us
and please Do come to stay.
I don't know how that we'll survive
without your grand display.

Coaching Questions:

I. What positives did you find in this chapter? What challenged you?

II. What threats or obstacles often prevent your message from getting through?

III. What is the message that the Lord is ultimately striving to speak through you?

IV. What has been your connection to the Holy Spirit?

V. How do you need to align your voice more with the Spirit?

Speaking Exercises:

I. Describe an experience where you listened to a powerful speaker and experienced the presence of God.

II. In one minute, describe the Spirit of Christ.

III. Describe how a speaker can be aligned and sensitive to the Spirit of God.

IV. Describe some internal barriers a speaker might have to overcome so that the Spirit of Christ can abound in his or her voice.

Chapter 9: Identifying the Falsehoods

One trailblazing dung beetle
Crosses the quiet desert path
And rolls his circular ball forward
Looking for safe sands to nest.

Pressing on the long journey
His mate catches up to him and
Scurries to help him bury the dung ball
Into the soft earth to insert her egg.

Birthed into a bundle of dung
And maturing past youth
The young adult flies back to the heap
Landing on the pile of guile.

The approaching storm clouds
Darken the horizon
And as the tempest begins to swirl
The beetle is thrown into darkness.

The long parade of distant followers
Flying to their new home
Are scattered to the furious storm.

Rise of the Plagues

Early the next morning, Moses is called upon by the Lord to give Pharaoh a "wake up call" by sending the first plague—a harbinger of the coming swarm of chaos.

As the sun rose across the Nile, the Lord instructed Moses to go and meet Pharaoh to show just how serious He was about delivering His people:

> You shall say to him, "The Lord, the God of the Hebrews, sent me to you, saying, 'Let My people go, that they may serve Me in the wilderness. But behold, you have not listened until now.' Thus says the Lord, 'By this you shall know that I am the Lord: behold, I will strike the water that is in the Nile with the staff that is in my hand,

and it will be turned to blood. The fish that are in the Nile will die, and the Nile will become foul, and the Egyptians will find difficulty in drinking water from the Nile.'" (Exodus 7:16–18)

The hand of the Lord started the first of nine powerful plagues by striking hard at the source—their system of transportation, water reserve, and religious foundation. Moses instructed Aaron to raise his staff over the Nile and the main water supply in Egypt turned to blood. As the fish of the Nile perished, a heavy cloud of uncertainty fell upon Egypt. For seven days, the water was undrinkable so that the people had to dig around the Nile for water (Exodus 7:19–24).

The Nile, the longest river in the world, provided (then and now) a significant flow of silty nutrients from the mountain rains in East Africa. These rains nurture the rich soils, and the dark nutrients flood the River Valley each year to support wheat for food, flax for clothing, and papyrus for writing. A breakdown of the Nile river translated to a breakdown in Egypt's economy and their way of life.

More than just a river, the Nile for Egypt was a fountain of folklore from which their religious system was built. Much of their worship and reverence was aimed at the "creature gods" that emerged from the Nile. Disrupting the Nile was the Lord's way of confronting their belief system and providing insight into His powerful Character, Identity, and Strength.

Why provide a lesson about this unique river? More than just a geography lesson, there's a metaphor here about finding our voice.

How the river springs is how the river rings.

When we are developing our voice—sweet, sour, or in between—the health of its origin influences the vitality of the message. The heart and the soul of the messenger are the source from where our message comes forth. **Are we bringing forth a spirit of truth and life, or is our soul marred by falsehoods, lies, and self-deceits that could impair our reach?**

Put another way, how our message is "earthed" is how it is "girthed."

Let's search out and discover the beginnings which originate our voice.

The quality of our soul is foundational to who we are. Pastor John Ortberg compares the soul of a man to a mountain stream that feeds his heart, mind, and strength[1]. Our souls are the "operating system" that integrates all our systems and is the seat of the spirit of man, which gives us our very breath.

Underneath the words, the message and the bravado, what is driving your voice? Are you speaking from love? Or the desire for power? Jealousy perhaps? Control?

---

[1] Taken from *Soul Keeping* by Pastor John Ortberg (2014).

In this chapter, we drive down and examine the under-currents, beliefs, potential strongholds, values, truths, and even falsehoods that prescribe the vibe.

There's an amazing principle in the Bible that reveals the seeds we plant bring up the crops we harvest. If we plant wheat, we are *not* going to harvest squash. If we plant squash, we are not going to reap corn.

> **Do not be deceived, God is not mocked;**
> **for whatever one sows, that will he also reap. (Galatians 6:7, ESV)**

In the same way, *if we plant the seeds of faith, hope, and love, the yield is a harvest of fruitful lives grounded in truth.* Conversely, if we plant criticism, oppression, and control, the harvest is depression, despair, and destructive relationships.

Ironically, the word "mocked" used in this passage is rooted in the mooing sounds of lowing animals and their snout. The word literally means "to turn up the nose or sneer at." So, the message is this: Turn up your nose and sneer at God's plan at your own risk.

In the case of Pharaoh, let's call it "reaper-concussions."

After his empire dished out 400 years of oppression, slavery, torment, and suffering, Egypt's own harvest will come in so strong that we are still talking about it 3,000 plus years later.

What about your origins? How have the "roots" in your life influenced your voice? Moreover, where do the "roots" need uncovering and refining?

Painted Gods and Rock Portraits

When Moses first returned to his old stomping grounds, the culture of Egypt's religious system must have hit him like a ton of mud bricks. During his upbringing in the royal courts, he was immersed in the worship of a multitude of gods: Ra, Isis, Osiris, and many more. The Pharaoh of the day also considered himself a high god.

In addition, there was a diverse and sizable array of priests, many of them with different types of roles and functions. The priests' roles varied from monitoring the astrological signs, to writing religious texts, to maintaining local temples, to managing the huge responsibilities of handling the journey from death to the afterlife.

The sacred god Khepri (with a beetle's head upon a man's body) was often worshipped upon a short obelisk with a stone dung beetle astride the top.

Though not as powerful nor as prominent as some of Egypt's other deities, the focus on Khepri shows both Egypt's obsession with death and fascination with bugs. The countless throng of small creatures stationed on the banks of the Nile were considered protectors and guardians of this river of life.

This sacred dung beetle was placed upon the amulet and given to those (in the multitudes) who passed from this life. This god served under the sun god by helping him carry the sun across the sky, similar to the way that the dung beetle rolled their circular balls of dung across the ground—as seen in this bizarre chapter opening.

Wait, though! There's a problem with this concept. The sun, as we now know, is not carried across the sky by another god and not by the manifestation of the determined, albeit disturbing, dung beetle. Rather, the earth revolves around the sun.

Oops.

Their ideal model of worship was backwards. *The focus needs to be on the Son!*

Nevertheless, before we start to take them to task, let's consider:
- Have we ever had some misunderstandings about God?
- Have we ever found ourselves confused, owning a lie or falsehood?
- Which falsehoods or misunderstandings undermine our lives?

For years of my life, I held on to my own self-deception. That is, I deceived myself by really thinking I was powerless to do anything about my speaking problems. Upgrading my voice was not an option because I never saw a way past the problem.

In the same way, we can "warp our own reality" by holding on to these "false-hoods." That is, we have eye-coverings that keep us from seeing life as it really is.

Have you ever found yourself lying to yourself?

Some of these attitudes are subtle and speak softly, but they have a powerful impact by holding us back from pressing forward. Some of these attitudes are like heavy chains and strongholds that keep us in the past.

A Series of Devastating Plagues

After 400 years of bitter enslavement and cruel oppression of the Hebrews... After building a lifestyle centered around a religious system that detested anything to do with the God of Moses, Abraham, and Jacob... The day of reckoning arrived for Egypt in full force. In the next 3 chapters of the Bible, Exodus 8–10, the Lord unleashes a series of plagues that devastate their economy, puts a dagger in their swagger, and even puts boils on the backs of their starry-eyed priests.

Within the scope of our focus on finding our voice, we are choosing only to hit the highlights—or rather, the lowlights—of these events, with the understanding that they were a direct consequence of oppressing Israel and worshipping false gods.

(If you love studying about apocalyptic events, you can go deeper into these traumatic events when you have time.)

In addition, Moses and Aaron were asked repeatedly by the Lord to either talk to Pharaoh, or to visually demonstrate these signs from a distance so that the dictator could clearly see that they were coming from Yahweh Himself. Remember that Yahweh is the Old Testament Hebrew name for the God of the Bible.

Generally the pattern of confrontation followed this way: Moses warning, Pharaoh ignoring, the plague roaring, and the people mourning. Each was followed by Pharaoh relenting briefly, only to harden his heart again after the plague ceased.

Here's a list of the next eight plagues:

The Plague of Frogs (Exodus 8:1–15),
When the innumerable frogs even went into Pharaoh's bed.
The Plague of Gnats/Insects (Exodus 8:16–22),
When Egypt's priests couldn't reproduce the plague, saying: "This is the finger of God." (v. 19)
The Plague of Flies (Exodus 8:23–32),
When Pharaoh tried to barter with Moses and receive a reprieve.
The Plague of Livestock Dying (Exodus 9:1–7),
When the cattle, the horses, and even all the camels died.
The Plague of Boils (Exodus 9:8–17),
When even the magicians were struck all over by boils.
The Plague of Hail (Exodus 9:18–34),
When Egypt's huge agricultural industry took a devastating blow.
The Plague of Locusts (Exodus 10:1–20),
When even Pharaoh's servants pleaded for Israel's cause.
The Plague of Intense Darkness (Exodus 10:21–19),
When Pharaoh almost buckled, but then changed his mind.

After the 9th plague and before the final strike, Pharaoh warned Moses to never come back into his presence or he would surely die! Indeed, Moses agreed that this would be the last time they would likely ever meet face to face (Exodus 10:28–29).

The Swarm

Swarm of fury
Swarm of flies
The swarm of frogs croak and die.

"Pharaoh let my people go
Bring us freedom tomorrow.
Our God on High will rise and strike
Let our people take our flight."

Swarm of gnats and locusts chomp
Chewing up the grass and crops
Mulch the harvest into dust—
To the Promised Land or Bust.

Boils upon your butts and brow
Fester wounds so red and raw
Disease to strike your cattle too
A curse upon the mooing zoo.

"Pharaoh let my people go
Bring us freedom tomorrow.
Our God on High will rise and strike
Let our people take our flight."

Hail will come and drop like thunder
The fires fall so gaze in wonder
Then the darkness falls on down
Melt in awe at His strong crown.

Who can stand against the storm?
Fright and strife become the swarm.
The land which once made other's troubles
Has fallen into calm and rubble.

"Pharaoh let my people go
Bring us freedom tomorrow.
Our God on High will rise and strike
Let our people take our flight."

Call the Deep-Cleaning Exterminator

What an overwhelming message the Lord sends to show Himself— His power, His authority, His dominance, and His desire to restore His people. Furthermore, how proud the heart of Pharaoh to resist at every possible cost. His oppressive "voice" (*No Way God!*) significantly impacted those under his leadership.

The Lord took particular exception to their obsession with bugs and beetles and gave them the very outcome and harvest of what they had worshipped for ages.

The implied message behind the plague:

You love bugs...I'll give you bugs!

Still, Egypt is not the only people or country that focuses on the small distractions. Let's bring this closer to home. In fact, *we* also get easily distracted by not giving the Lord His rightful place as King of the Universe. Let's use an acronym, "PEST":

P - Pitfalls
E - Emerging from
S - Subverting
T - Truth

"Pests" are those wrongful influences that subvert the truth about who we are in relationship to God and who we are in relationship to one another. These "pests" divert our focus, distract our faith, and undermine our forward progress.

A swarm of bees can take down a grizzly bear.

Falsehoods About Who God Is

We're going to break down these pest-like falsehoods into 2 types: Falsehoods about who God is, and falsehoods about our own identity and abilities.

Frequently, when we are first coming to know God to establish a relationship with Him, we have misconceptions about His identity and purpose. For example, some of these misconceptions are that:

- God is like a weak old man who reigns with a long beard.
- God is like a policeman who just wants to throw us in "jail" to punish us.
- God is like a distant pushover who seldom gets involved in the life events of men.
- God is remote enough to adjust to my agenda, and not mine to his.

Who is God, really? How can we know Him intimately when He is strong enough to create an entire Universe? Does He really care about our lives and the struggles of humanity?

The Bible calls Him:
Powerful Creator (Genesis 1:1, Isaiah 48:20)
Uplifting King (Psalm 97:1, Psalm 47:7)
Loving Father (1 John 4:8, Psalm 103:13)
Visionary Leader (Ecclesiastes 3:11, Revelation 21)
…and much more.

God is big enough that He does not really have to explain Himself, but He chooses to reveal Himself through His Son Jesus. He is wise, and compassionate (Psalm 103:4), and His understanding has no limit (Psalm 147:5).

The heart and passion of God is for us. In fact, the apostle Paul declares:

If God be for us, who can be against us? If He did not spare His own son, what blessing will he withhold? (Romans 8:31–32, Author's Paraphrase)

From this chapter and this entire turn of reckoning events, we can certainly see that God takes sin, unbelief, and rebellion seriously, but He doesn't relish in the choices people make to reject Him. The Lord does not celebrate when people lose their way (Ezekiel 33:11). In fact, the Father uses the consequences of rebellion to bring us around to His redemptive cause.

If you're struggling to find God's identity, let me encourage you to search Him out. The Lord says:

You will seek Me and find Me when you search for Me with all your heart. (Jeremiah 29:13)

Search out His character, His heart, His plans, and His purposes for your life.

Falsehoods About Our Own Identities and Abilities

Accepting negative beliefs about ourselves is like allowing weeds in the harvest fields. These "weeds" pollute our minds, bodies, and souls with reeking thinking and destructive desires that undermine fruitfulness.

As we explore the deeper wellspring, let's ask ourselves:
Is there any part of me that:
- *Holds on to the idea that my voice has no reason to be heard?*
- *Limits my beliefs that I can connect with friends or build community?*
- *Hampers my confidence of speaking effectively?*
- *Undermines my dreams and aspirations about a bright future?*

In regard to our relationships, deeper feelings can still be expressed in unconventional ways. Even the power of touch overrides mere words. Hugs, comfort, and affection express caring that is felt even down to the soul.

Friends can meet relational needs that are often unspoken or given with just a relatively short amount of words, such as:

- Attention—just being there and providing the power of presence.
- Appreciation—just telling someone, "I appreciate you."
- Respect—giving others the value they merit as friends.
- Support—meeting their needs such as yardwork, laundry, etc.
- Comfort—expressing care and concerns, often with no words at all.

Growing in the area of speaking with loving affection certainly will strengthen our relationships. Great communication spills into every area of each relationship.

How do we counter the lies? Let's get to the root...and to the source.

What's at the root of these subversive lies?

In order to remove them completely we must get at the source:

> Have the lies come from negative influences from our family?
>
> Have the falsehoods come from our work, community, or church?

When we "drink" of a faulty source and we allow negative influences to infiltrate and to soak into the lining of our souls, we are going to reap a harvest of sick crops.

Building a healthy speaking community is so important to expose these dark strongholds. A stronghold is a fortress of faulty belief that builds up walls and keeps us from walking in the truth.

In the case of Egypt, the Lord brought a harvest soaked in death. The smell of the Nile turning to blood alone confronted their physical senses. Then there was the smell of the dead fish, followed by the multitudes of piles of dead frogs. Can you imagine after all the cattle and livestock died how badly the country must have smelled?

Yet in all these plagues, the Hebrew people were spared. Jesus himself says:

But whoever drinks the water I give them will never thirst. Indeed, the water I give them will become in them a spring of water welling up to eternal life. (John 4:14, NIV)

The words of Christ are sweet and life-giving words.

Jesus' promises are a solid foundation to withstand storms (Matthew 7:24–27).

Jesus' words are the words of truth (John 14:6).

Jesus' words and promises never fade away as He says:

> **Heaven and earth will pass away**
> ***but my words will never pass away.*** **(Matt 24:35)**

Therefore, when we place Jesus at the center of our lives, not only does our perspective change, but Christ changes our hearts from the inside out. Then our voice is empowered with peace, strength, and confidence.

How Hard Times Give Your Voice Texture

Before we head into the coaching questions, consider this: Moses received the most opportunities to speak during his most difficult days. Public speakers need practice, and Moses picked up many opportunities.

All in all, Moses went before Pharaoh ten times to advocate for freedom.

How did these hard times affect Moses' clarity of message to Pharaoh?

How did these hard times affect *the way Moses spoke* the message?

What happened to Moses' faith during this "war in the heavenlies"?

Hard times give our message "texture" to help our voice grow stronger and more resolute. Hard times give our tone more endurance and perseverance. Hard times are the very thing that helps to uncover weaknesses, barriers, unbelief, and relational gaps.

Once again, **underneath the words, the message and the bravado, what is driving your voice?** Are you speaking from faith? Or love? Or the desire for power? Jealousy? Control?

What negative influences are tainting your voice and painting your future with clouds from the past?

Surrender them to the Lord.

Hold on to your faith.

Freedom is not far away.

Stand on the only threads of courage you have left.

Coaching Questions:

I. What positives did you find this chapter? What challenged you?
II. In what areas of your life have you struggled with self-deception?
III. What are the PESTs or small distractions that keep you from knowing God?
IV. What areas of your worship to God have been "backwards"? That is, where have you misunderstood or held on to falsehoods about who God really is?
V. How have your misunderstandings with God affected your relationship with Him?
VI. In what areas do you struggle with accepting your own speaking limitations?
VII. If you're holding on to any falsehoods about your abilities/service, how are you going to confront these and move past them?

Speaking Exercises:

I. Share an example of self-deception, like the author has, that you have struggled with.
II. Share how the hard times in life have affected your voice.
III. If you are so bold, share where you are laying "eggs birthed in dung" or "dreams birthed in deception."

Chapter 10: The Power of Sacrificial Love

Two solitary men walk the remote path,
    Traversing slowly from opposite directions at dusk.
Pausing, they glance into one another's haggard eyes.
    The desperation runs deep.

        After the scourge, the cattle were gone.
        After the hail, the grain was gone.
        Still, after the locusts,
        There was nothing left.

"Anything to eat?" one grumbles to the other.
    "Catch a fish or surely die," follows the reply.
"When will the Hebrews leave this land?"
    "Soon, I hope. Or how will we ever last?"

        After the scourge, the cattle were gone.
        After the hail, the grain was gone.
        Still, after the locusts,
        There was nothing left.

Departing they sluggishly wander off together.
    Slipping away in the distance,
The moment quickly passes as
    The day like vapor fast escapes.

        Their silhouettes fade into a receding sunset.[1]

---

1 Theme taken from Joel, Chapter 1.

A Terrible Fright at Midnight

How heartbreaking to live through this devastating season. How exhausting these plagues must have been. How many thousand Egyptians must have died? While we do not have exact numbers, every single soul who falls is a true loss. In the final days, the Egyptians themselves were more than ready to see Israel evacuate, saying, "We will all die" (Exodus 12:33, NIV). However, in the Land of Goshen where Israel lived, the people avoided destruction. Their hearts were filled with anticipation with every passing punch at their oppressors.

Egypt's troubles are not over, though. The final deliverance for the Hebrews is going to come at an extremely high price for Pharaoh. The number ten (10) in Biblical usage is often a symbol of completion. The last plague upon the land is the 10th plague, and the most awe-striking yet.

The place of the firstborn in ancient Mid-Eastern times was important. The firstborn would receive the lion's share of the inheritance and most of the status in the father's family estate. The Lord calls the nation of Israel his firstborn; and since Egypt has oppressed them, the Egyptians will pay a huge price at the expense of their firstborn children. The Lord gives Moses these instructions next:

Speak to all the congregation of Israel, saying, "On the tenth of this month they are each one to take a lamb for themselves, according to their fathers' households, a lamb for each household." (Exodus 12:3)

The Lord gives Moses specific instructions to make sure the lamb is unblemished, roasted, and then eaten with bitter herbs. He instructs the people to put the Lamb's blood over their doorposts as a sign of deliverance (Exodus 12:5–10).

Pay attention to directions, Moses. Listen as your life depends on this.
Our lives will depend upon this.
The Lord continues his instructions:

Now you shall eat it in this manner: with your loins girded, your sandals on your feet, and your staff in your hand; and you shall eat it in haste—it is the Lord's Passover. For I will go through the land of Egypt on that night, and will strike down all the firstborn in the land of Egypt, both man and beast; and against all the gods of Egypt I will execute judgments—I am the Lord. The blood shall be a sign for you on the houses where you live; and when I see the blood I will pass over you, and no plague will befall you to destroy you when I strike the land of Egypt. (Exodus 12:11–13)

This worst plague is yet to come. Death is about to pay your town a visit; in the final judgment of Revelation, he will come on a pale horse and arrive in the same fashion (Revelation 6:8).

The Lord Himself says He is behind this, but He comes in the form of death and judgment. He will strike the firstborn in every home, on every corner, and even in every cattle stall in Egypt.

This time the plague will even pay a visit to Goshen where the Hebrews live.

What will spare the nation of Israel from certain destruction?

Only this: The blood of the lamb.

The lamb is a portrait of lowly and gentle innocence.

When John the Baptist first announced the arrival of Jesus, he declared, "*Behold, the Lamb of God who takes away the sin of the world*" (John 1:29).

Our Biblical principle in Chapter 10 is:

In the Lamb's sacrifice is beautiful deliverance, just as sacrificial love has the power to change lives.

Notice in the Exodus passage, the lamb needs to be "unblemished." That is, the sacrifice needs to be in prime condition, because a defective lamb is no sacrifice at all.

By faith, we understand that Christ is the pure sacrifice—acceptable to God. Jesus puts it this way:

Greater love has no one than this, that one lay down his life for his friends. You are My friends if you do what I command you. No longer do I call you slaves, for the slave does not know what his master is doing; but I have called you friends, for all things that I have heard from My Father I have made known to you. You did not choose Me but I chose you, and appointed you that you would go and bear fruit, and that your fruit would remain. (John 15:13–16)

More than just speaking truth, there's power in living out the example of Christ and expressing the beauty of sacrifice. Jesus lived out this example by sacrificing Himself for the sins of the world (John 10:11).

Is Anybody Listening to Me? Can Anyone Really Understand?

Century after century dragged on for a million plus Hebrew slaves. The relentless pain and unceasing tide of torment from slavery cut deeply to their core. The national clamor echoed out for years. Is anybody listening? Can anybody hear?

The Lord's first words to Moses speak comfort. Here they are again:

I have surely seen the affliction of My people who are in Egypt, and have given heed to their cry because of their taskmasters, for I am aware of their sufferings. (Exodus 3:7)

So much encouragement comes from knowing how the God of the Bible is intimately aware of the suffering and sorrow of His people. He has compassion upon the hurting. He knows their pain and knows exactly what they are going through. He understands their plight. He has a plan to restore them and to deliver them.

His Plan is the Lamb.

The unblemished Lamb is a direct response to their biggest challenge—not the hubris of Pharaoh, but rather the pride and corruption of their own hearts! Sin runs in the family. Wrongdoing is at the core of the human heart.

Without paying the price, there is no mercy. Distinctly, the Bible says that:

Without the shedding of blood there is no forgiveness of sins. (Hebrews 9:22b, ESV)[2]

In Exodus 12, The Lord told Moses for each household to take the lamb (v. 3) and:
- Kill it at twilight (v. 6).
- Take some of the blood and put it over the doorposts (v. 7).
- Eat the flesh that same night (v. 8).

What was the Lord's purpose?

The Lord is providing a true covering for the people. The Lord is protecting them from the penalty and the punishment for idolatry and wrongdoing.

The innocent lamb is the substitute receiving the punishment for their sin.

The blood is the outcome of the sacrifice.

Sinfulness and brokenness are ultimately messy. Watching the death of the lamb reminds the people of the messiness, high cost, and disruption of their own sins.

How does the "sin problem" relate to finding our voice?

The "sin problem" is what separates us from God, from others, and even from ourselves. This sin problem skews our focus and bottlenecks our growth.

Jesus declares that **"everyone who sins is a slave to sin"** (John 8:34, NIV). In a sense, we're all slaves. We're all "chained" to our selfish nature that puts ourselves above others.

Our sin must be placed upon Jesus and upon the cross to cover the debt.

---

[2] See also Leviticus 17:11, Ephesians 1:7, and Romans 5:9-11.

Why take sinfulness seriously? Because God takes it seriously. Dead serious.

However, there's great news! The Word says, when we confess our sins, He is faithful and merciful to forgive us and to clean us from all unworthy acts (1 John 1:9).

The Father is a keeper of justice, as He allows for consequences for wicked acts; but the Father is also merciful, putting His own Son on the cross to pay the price for our sin.

I know, I know. This sounds a little preachy and snooty.

But...the Word of God calls us **all** *out for our sins. I'm not calling you out for this, I'm calling out my own weakness and my own sinfulness.*

Without Christ, I'm sunk, but His eternal love makes a way through.

Empowering Your Voice

Sacrificial love is what makes the voice of a leader beautiful.

Don't miss out on the most powerful part of the story. Turn your ears up.

When your life serves as a sacrifice for those in your community, they cannot help but notice.

I've been asking a lot of difficult questions throughout the narrative, but one of the most difficult is this:

Do
You
Love
The
People
You are
Speaking to?

Really, do you love and care for the people in your community who need your voice? Or is speaking merely an exercise to blow your own horn and to tout your credentials? Do you have a deep and unconditional love that builds bridges?

We are not going to judge you if your motivations are not focused on others, but we *really do* want to encourage you to consider how much more impactful your message will be with unconditional love.

More than just speaking love...your voice is about showing love.

Let your actions back up your message.

If I speak with the tongues of men and of angels, but do not have love, I have become a noisy gong or a clanging cymbal. If I have the gift of prophecy, and know all mysteries and all knowledge; and if

I have all faith, so as to remove mountains, but do not have love, I am nothing. And if I give all my possessions to feed the poor, and if I surrender my body to be burned, but do not have love, it profits me nothing. (1 Corinthians 13:1–3)

Expressly, the Lord wants to transport His love through you and toward your broken community.

When Jesus walked the earth and reached out to a broken community, His first concern was not their sickness or diseases, but the condition of their souls and their broken relationships with God.

To the woman who is caught up in a broken lifestyle, Jesus says, "Your sins have been forgiven" (Luke 7:48).

Where are the broken relationships in your community?

Where is the hurting and where is the loss?

Where is the guilt and the pain?

The Lamb of God, Jesus Himself, has the power to cleanse and to forgive. That power changes *both* the speaker and the audience.

The speaker is freed up to inspire and transform lives by the Spirit of Christ.

The audience is awakened and empowered to renew their lives afresh.

Final Hours In Egypt

Just imagine the anticipation on the night of escape.

What does freedom taste like? How does it feel?

The people could only guess.

Now it came about at midnight that the Lord struck all the firstborn in the land of Egypt, from the firstborn of Pharaoh who sat on his throne to the firstborn of the captive who was in the dungeon, and all the firstborn of the cattle. Pharaoh arose in the night, he and all his servants and all the Egyptians, and there was a great cry in Egypt, for there was no home where there was not someone dead." (Exodus 12:29–30)

Midnight is the time that one day ends and a new day begins. Midnight, on this occasion, is the completion of 400 years of oppression.

The new day springs like a geyser gushing at great speed!

The Lord strikes hard at Israel's oppressors, striking down the first born of the highest in the land, the King himself, as well as the lowest in the land in prison. Even the "cattle" were affected. But wait, didn't the cattle already get taken out? The word for "cattle" in this passage is literally "beast" in the original language. The Bible says that even the remaining beasts of the fields were affected by this plague.

What was the reaction? A "great cry" rose out of Egypt as every family was affected. Literally, an "outcry" rose up and Pharaoh finally felt the pressure to do something about their predicament. Without even waiting for morning, Pharaoh summoned Moses and Aaron to come and spoke:

Then he called for Moses and Aaron at night and said, "Rise up, get out from among my people, both you and the sons of Israel; and go, worship the Lord, as you have said. Take both your flocks and your herds, as you have said, and go, and bless me also." (Exodus 12:31–32)

There comes a point where even our worst enemies surrender. Faced with the death of his own son, a plague upon everyone's house, and the outcry of the nation, Pharaoh finally relents. *"Rise up...get out...go...worship...take your herds...and bless me also" (Exodus 12:32).*

Goodbye Moses, good riddance.

Don't let the blood-stained door hit you on the way out.

And "bless me also"? Wait, what?

Why is Pharaoh asking for a blessing? Begrudgingly he must admit to God's power and incredible work.

More than just providing a way out of Egypt, the Lord establishes a major holiday, sacred observance, and powerful reminder of His faithfulness, strength, and character through the Passover (see Exodus 12:14–21). He instructed His people to celebrate this meal (with unleavened bread) each year to commemorate this Passover.

Moses' leadership stock in the nation of Israel has suddenly gone through the roof. His voice echoes through the community, but this time his message is like an unforgettable breakthrough of beaming light bursting through the doors.

Pack your bags, family of God!

Bid your neighbors farewell.

Kiss. This. Scorched earth. Goodbye.

With their flocks in tow, their few belongings, their neighbors' plunder, and their unleavened dough, the 600,000 men and their families left Egypt and found freedom.

This liberated nation will never be the same.

Unconditional Sacrifice Makes a Difference

The sacrifice of the lamb and the Passover for Israel have a direct correlation for Christ, His followers, and for the church.

Jesus Himself took on the role of the Lamb.

God made **"Him who knew no sin to be sin on our behalf, so that we might become the righteousness of God in Him"** (2 Corinthians 5:21).

Jesus offers eternal freedom and forgiveness.

So, if the Son sets you free, you will be free indeed. **(John 8:36, NIV)**

Call it Freedom with a capital F.

More than just giving forgiveness and freedom, the Lamb understands our joys, our fears, our sadness, and even our pain. His presence is freedom and grace.

Now the Lord is the Spirit,
    and where the Spirit of the Lord is, there is freedom. **(2 Corinthians 3:17, NIV)**

Have you experienced this Freedom?

Have you dealt with the heavy weight of your sin, and found lasting forgiveness?

More importantly, have you considered a relationship with the Lord and how this freedom can impact your message as a leader?

Once we have encountered Christ and His Spirit touches our lives, our message takes on a new tone and new flow.

By God's grace, we are more willing to serve and to sacrifice for our community out of gratitude and deep appreciation.

In the book of Revelation, we discover that "the Lamb was slain from the foundation of the world" (Revelation 13:8, NIV). That is, from the very beginning of creation, the Heavenly Father knew how He would solve the "sin problem" by sending His Son Jesus.

The Bible says that the mercies of God are lifegiving (Ephesians 2:4–5) and "new every morning" (Lamentations 3:23). His Spirit pours into us by faith with love, joy, peace, patience, kindness, gentleness, goodness, faithfulness and even self-control (Galatians 5:22–23).

Does the Sin Count Climb Every Day?

Back in about 2012, I heard an experienced pastor friend pose the question, "How many times do you sin in a day?" Nobody had ever posed such a question to our Arizona church plant before, and I had never considered this thought myself.

"Do not include your bad thoughts," the leader said, "Nor sins of lapse where you missed opportunities. Let's just say three," he declared.

That's a modest number to start with.

Our Pastor friend started adding up the numbers, stating that with three sins a day, at 300 days plus a year, that's roughly 1,000 sins per year. Then, if we live 65 to 70 years, the potential total adds up to 65,000 to 70,000 sins.

Wow. I had never added up the total before.

Are we starting to understand and to feel the burdensome weight of our sins?

Even minor sins separate us from a Perfect, Holy, Awesome, Glorious God. To be "holy" means to be "set apart for a sacred purpose." What if my total sin count is 64,389 and your total is 62,782? *Indeed, we both are sinners needing grace!*

Who can Save us from these scandalous stains?

Jesus Christ—who came to seek and to save that which was LOST.

The resurrection of Christ gives us the power to overcome our wrongful past (Colossians 1:19–20).

How to Sacrifice for Your Community?

Out of this close relationship with Christ, our voice takes on the powerful message of redemption, grace, freedom, and hope. So, how does this "power to forgive" in Christ transform your community? How can you walk in this grace to show unconditional love and sacrifice to your neighbors and bring hope to your "local predicament"?

Often, when we use the word sacrifice, we're thinking about money. You're already wondering what finances may be involved in engaging your community.

Let me gracefully suggest, there are many other ways to give yourself away:
- Giving your time to interact with struggling people
- Praying for your community
- Giving your heart to shepherd lives
- Giving your gifts and talents

The most beautiful sacrifice is this: Giving your very heart for others. The life and voice centered around the self is shallow. The life of sacrifice impacts others far more deeply.

For some, their gift is cooking, or constructing, or comforting. For others, they can craft music, or provide health care in troubling times.

Because Jesus sacrificed Himself for us, we sacrifice for others.

We love, because He first loved us. *(1 John 4:19)*

Aaron Remembers the First Day

Walking out of Egypt

We are finally free, Moses.
Thank our God and King.
I remember when I first reunited with you in the wilderness.
You struggled to confront Pharaoh,
And worried about your stammering tongue.
Your doubts arose and your fears ran strong.
When Pharaoh first rejected us,
Our souls fell deep into depression.

Still, you never gave up.
You embraced the vision to stand for freedom,
And faced down the tyrant.
When God spoke through you, you found confidence.
You have found your value as His chosen servant.
Our people now look to you as our leader.
Look how far you have come!

Consider, Moses, no more the past.
Move out forward into the blessed future.

Coaching Questions:

I. What positives did you find in this chapter? What challenged you?

II. What do the events surrounding the Lamb's sacrifice tell us about the character of God?

III. How do you think Moses reacted to the news of freedom?

IV. Where can the eternal love of Christ make a difference in your relationship with Him (e.g., vision, endurance, patience, forgiveness, peace)?

V. How can the power of sacrifice, in the Lamb Jesus, transform your relationships with friends and family?

VI. How can the power of Jesus' sacrificial love transform your community?

VII. Specifically, what are some ways you can serve and sacrifice for your community?

Speaking Exercises:

I. Describe a leader or positive influence in your life who has sacrificed for you unconditionally. What impact has this had on your life?

II. Share a struggle in your life of sin and how God's grace made a difference.

III. Describe for your group what the "first day of freedom" must have felt like for those walking out of slavery in Egypt.

Chapter 11: Stepping Into Your Rhythm

Voices.
Have you ever heard so many voices?
Facebook voices.
Twitter voices.
"Give us justice" voices.
"Everybody-speak-their-piece" voices.
The ranters.
The chanters.
The incredible banter.
I am _____ [fill in the blank]. Hear me roar!

So how is your voice going to be unique, distinctive and clear in all the uproar?

How are you going to make your voice count?

Great news.

You are not alone. By aligning with Jesus, you will strengthen your message, make your voice stand out by His unique Spirit, and widen your impact. Your Chosen to Speak family is here for you as well. We're developing new coaches all the time and establishing a network of leaders who care. Jesus said:

Heaven and earth will pass away
but my words will never pass away. (Matthew 24:35, NIV)

Therefore, when we are aligned with his Eternal Purposes and Plans, we can see our voices echo through generations with Spirit of God Staying Power.

Taking Inventory from the Story

What's the real takeaway from Moses' life, reflecting specifically on his speech impediments? Let's summarize key points from the narrative:

- Moses gave himself permission to face his speech obstacles.
- He turned his heart to listen deeply and to follow God's way.
- Moses denied himself by surrendering his pride to do the Father's will.
- More than just growing as a speaker, Moses grew as a dynamic leader.

In surrendering to God's will, Moses was given wisdom to speak to the nation.

The Hand of God delivered the nation as they found deliverance in the Lamb.

Moses' life was transformed by placing his value and his identity in his relationship with God and not trusting merely in his abilities or skills.

We also see from a very practical level that Moses was able to find his voice by repeatedly standing before Pharaoh to stand up for their cause. Getting enough "reps" is a real part of the process of developing as a speaker.

The more we can hone and refine our leadership, the more we can mature in sharing our voice and our story.

For we all stumble in many ways. If anyone does not stumble in what he says, he is a perfect man, able to bridle the whole body as well. (James 3:2)

The word "perfect" is literally the idea of being "complete" or mature. The writer James affirms that, in order to become mature in our life, we need to mature in our use of the tongue. Exercising good usage of the tongue helps to deploy the body as well.

Do you have a mature, complete voice?

In this chapter, let's focus on evaluating ourselves on how we can progress toward a complete, developed voice. The experienced leader with a voice that has been developed is in a better position to help develop the voices of others.

Fly on the Wall with the Coach

Coach Don picked up a drumstick.

"Now go ahead and start to teach. When you talk too fast, I'm going to hit the cymbal on this drum set," encouraged Don in a secluded church in 2013.

Bang.

Bang. Bang. Bang.

Bangbangbangbangbangbangbang.

Don slammed on the cymbals in rapid succession.

Bang.

Bang. Bang. Bang.

Bangbangbangbangbangbangbang.

"Dang. I get it. I talk too fast," I thought to myself.

"I'm really struggling to understand," said Don's pastor, Andrew.

This was somewhat embarrassing, to say the least.

For years I had heard people say, "You'll get used to it," referring to my rapid-fire speaking in public.

Now there's a moniker for speaking success: "Eventually mediocrity will settle in."

As Don started cranking on the cymbals at the speed of my speech, I was not surprised. Getting into the practice room was painful and problematic.

"But when you read the Bible verses, I can understand you," declared Don.

"Wait, what?!? There is something you actually like about my voice?"

After so many years of hearing so many negatives, it was a relief to hear something positive for a change—even if it was just something small.

Don continued that day to encourage me. "It's more difficult to change a speaking pattern than it is to quit smoking." He was essentially saying, "Don't quit. You can do this."

Wow.

So very few people had ever ventured into the fire to help with my delivery before.

"Work on your daily conversation," affirmed Don. "When you work on your pace within your relationships, you will improve your speaking in public."

Not only was I talking too fast—I knew that already. There were far too many words in most every sentence.

I had created a manuscript for each message, so I knew word counts and sentence lengths. Generally speaking, people process about 6 or 7 words at a time and then need a pause.

My sentences were more in the range of 10 to 12 words, and there was rarely any pausing. The combination of too many words at too fast a pace created a disruptive disconnect.

Coach Don Burns helped me to understand where the breakdown was.

On top of that, some of the words would mesh together into one word. "Word mesh" is the idea of joining two words together to form one, rending their meaning hazy. (This is still an issue for me in everyday conversation.)

I started to work on pacing during the week in conversations with others. This made a real difference. Thanks to the Lord's help and through repeated practice, there was a genuine turnaround.

Over time, I started to receive more positive feedback.

Finally, a "new normal" developed.

My audience understood more.

For those who struggle to find their voice, coaching is vital. Consistent feedback is imperative. More than just "one and done" counseling, our meetings went on for a series of months.

Are you willing to receive encouragement and counsel from your coach?

Finding Your Rhythm: In Calling

Like a musician who knows the vital importance of good timing, the good public speaker must find rhythm in his or her calling, relationships, heart life (emotional health), message content, and message delivery.

Let's review the question of "What's your calling?"

Having a clear vision of what the good Lord created you to do is vital.

Have you learned to listen to God's voice and discern what direction He has for you?

Sometimes we put that calling on hold.

Others have walked away from their calling. Maybe that's you?

Let me encourage you. Pursue your calling and discover what the Lord has for you to do on planet earth. You're not here by accident.

Finding Your Rhythm: In Relationships

Learning to love God and to love others takes intentionality.

Making a priority of spending time with God is at the heart of learning how to receive love and to give love.

Beloved, let us love one another, for love is from God; and everyone who loves is born of God and knows God. The one who does not love does not know God, for God is love. (1 John 4:7–8)

Let's take some time this week to spend with God and experience His love, grace, encouragement, wisdom and guidance. When we receive from Jesus, in relationship, we're able to pass encouragement and support on to others. The Apostle John continues this:

By this the love of God was manifested in us, that God has sent His only begotten Son into the world so that we might live through Him. (1 John 4:9)

Intimacy with God is the foundation for inspiring others to change.

Finding Your Rhythm: In Heart Life/Emotional Health

Do you know any capable guitarists that do not tune their guitars before leading or performing for others? Quality musicians tune their instruments well.

In the same way, let me challenge you and encourage you to turn your heart into the right instrument to speak and to empower your listeners.

Your heartbeat is the drum by which your passions inspire others.

Check your heart and examine yourself:
- What's your motive for speaking (to serve self or others)?
- Have you dealt with your fears before you speak?
- Do you harbor any guilt or anger or pride? Confess and surrender it.
- What about the pain? Are you renewing your heart and soul by the comfort and peace of God? Or are you still a walking wound?

Finding Your Rhythm: Message Content

Given the context, how do you organize the main idea of your message? Have you created an opening statement that provokes interest?
Is your main idea clear and concise?
Is your vision compelling enough for listeners to "buy in"?
Why would they want to bother with your message if you do not give them a strong reason to join in your new venture?
How can you get others involved in your dream if you are not willing to sacrifice yourself and invest your time and talents?
One of the most important parts of our message is the closing. Challenge people to live out the message in a practical way. Share your genuine love, hopes, and dreams for change.
Share your vision and message with your coach.
Have you given your listener some clear directions and important "next steps" so that you know if they are moving forward?
Later, we are going to spend time around the idea of organizing your message, developing your vision, and building your team to impact the community around you.

Finding Your Rhythm: Message Delivery

The perplexing matter of speaking is that we can be strong in all of the above areas and yet our verbal delivery could still hold us back.
Strong public speakers get about 5 to 7 words out at a time before pausing. With any more words, the listener is having to play catch up.
We live in a "soundbite culture" where the speaker boils his words down to what he ultimately has to say to connect.
Boil your message down. Then boil it down some more.
Can you articulate your dreams and passion in 3 minutes? One minute? How about one sentence? One phrase?
Think about some of the greatest speeches you have heard.
"Tear down this wall," from Reagan.
"We shall never surrender," from Churchill.
"I have a dream," from Martin Luther King.
Less. Is. Truly. More.

Moses' Inner Voice

As we were looking at Moses' life we observed his inferiorities. Consider what thoughts must have lurked under the surface about himself:

"Who am I when compared to the mighty Pharaoh?"

"How can I deliver Israel when I'm captive to my own fears?"

This is the sound of a man who has been telling himself for years how ineffective he has become. However, Moses faced his own failures in order to move forward.

Have we identified our own gaps and faced our failures?

Let's get to a level of deeper honesty.

Our confidence in the unshakable character and promises of God is the true anchor to build our lives upon.

One of my favorite verses is:

Anyone who believes in Him will never be put to shame. (Romans 10:11)

The Lord's calling and the Lord's love provide the depth of significance we are so hungry for. The Father reinforces this with the people He places in our lives.

The Father loves us with a *perfect love*.

What really is "perfect love"?

The Apostle John gives us this insight:

***There is no fear in love; but perfect love casts out fear, because fear involves punishment, and the one who fears is not perfected in love.* (1 John 4:18)**

Perfect love is God's deep, limitless, unconditional love.

Perfect love is complete, enduring love.

Perfect love has no fear.

His perfect love, given by His Spirit, directly drives out your fears. God's perfect love, working also through your coach and friends, drives out fear.

Our human love is incomplete and imperfect, but His love prevails.

When Words Get in the Way

This book, ***Chosen to Speak,*** is foundational in helping us to lay the groundwork for relationships and future service together. While the goal is to mature in our voice, we understand that this is a process.

This development track is an adventure and a journey that we want to walk on together. More than just a book to read and to gather dust, we pray that this will be a springboard to future growth in Christ and in friendship.

How can we have a complete voice without a mature love?

In the later years of Moses' life, he spoke these words to the Lord:

O satisfy us in the morning with Your loving kindness,
That we may sing for joy and be glad all our days. (Psalm 90:14)

Without the enduring love of God, Moses' story would never have unfolded.

My own little story would be impossible without the Lamb.

Yet by God's grace the journey is coming to an end.

Thanks for the diligence to take each step.

This is the end of one trek.

Let's start another.

Soon.

Unworthy

Lord, every day I get a clear glimpse of my own unworthiness.
  A bad hair day.
  A rumbling cough.
  Sometimes, I can't even remember where I put my shoes.
How can I walk worthy with you in life,
  when I can barely start the day until the fog lifts?

You are worthy, our Lord and God, to receive glory and honor and power, for you created all things, and by your will they ... have their being. (Revelation 4:11, NIV)

Lord, how can I live by your words when I'm so weak?
  One moment I cheer your praises and proclaim my love.
  The next I wander into selfish thinking.
  I live as if I am the only person alive.
Help me to see the big picture.
Your plans are bigger and you're establishing an eternal Kingdom.

Worthy is the Lamb, who was slain, to receive power and wealth and wisdom and strength and honor and glory and praise! (Revelation 5:12, NIV)

Jesus you are the author and the finisher of our faith.
Guide us. Refine us.
Polish us.
Mature us in faith and fulfill your full love.
Establish your vision and all your plans.
Spring up your life in us.

Coaching Questions:

I. What positives did you find in this chapter? What challenged you?

II. How would you define a "mature voice" in your own words?

III. Have you discovered what your clear calling from God is?

IV. In what ways has your heart life (emotional health) been a hindrance to your voice? What steps can you take to get on track?

V. What gaps in rhythm are there in your relationships, content, and delivery that keep you from making a strong impact?

VI. How can you start to build a team to impact your "local bondage" and community needs?

VII. In what area do you need to improve your speaking the most?

Speaking Exercises:

I. Share in three minutes your dream for a transformed community.

II. Share that dream in one minute.

III. Share it in one sentence. One phrase?

Chapter 12: Moving Forward in the Lord

1st Century Jerusalem:
Frantic.
Two anxious parents scurry back into Jerusalem
To search for their missing son after Passover.
The City is overflowing with the multitudes.

"Where could he be?" the mother shouts above the ruckus.
The major holiday has concluded and their
Only child, twelve years old, is unaccounted for.

Three. Agonizing days pass. Without a sign.

Did he make a new teenage friend
Or wander off looking for new adventure?
"Let's try looking in the Temple," persists the father.

In the midst of the crowd of onlookers
Young Jesus is speaking to the scribes,
Listening and asking questions.

The people are amazed at his insight.
His parents marvel in the moment and
Then ask, "Why have you treated us like this?"
Finally, they can breathe again.

Jesus shepherds his lost parents in public saying,
 "Didn't you know that I would be in my Father's house
 And doing the things of the Father?"

Mary and Joseph are perplexed.

On the long walk back home to Nazareth,
An awkward silence follows them.
From Luke 2:41–51.

Jesus' Uniqueness as a Public Speaker

Can you imagine how difficult those three long days were for Mary and Joseph, looking for Christ? Certainly they wondered where He would eat, sleep, and find shelter. Mystified, they must have questioned how this young leader could carry Himself for so long in the presence of the City's leading sages.

Jesus was not your typical twelve-year-old.

Even before He left home, He was exercising strong speaking gifts.

Jesus remains one of the most powerful speakers of all time. Who is stronger, really?

What characteristics in speaking made Him so extraordinary? Let's take a look.

Notice Jesus responds to His parents saying,

Why did you seek Me? Did you not know that I must be about My Father's business? (Luke 2:49, NKJV)

Jesus replies by essentially asking, "Where else would I be?"

Jesus' authority came from His Father (Matthew 28:18). His strength came through His willingness to obey and to follow His Father's will above all else, just as the Heavenly Father anointed Jesus efforts to build His reputation.

When the Father has your back, your speech makes an impact.

The Bible teaches that the Heavenly Father has a great passion for His Name and His Glory. We discover this in the teachings of Christ (Matthew 6:9, Isaiah 42:8).

Are you willing to follow the voice of the Heavenly Father?

Are you willing to do His Will?

What is God's will? That we know and believe in His Son!

Jesus prayed,

This is eternal life, that they may know You, the only true God, and Jesus Christ whom You have sent. (John 17:3)

Speak Like Jesus

Jesus' speaking voice is unique because He taught with authority and with power (Matthew 7:28–29). As a result of His commitment to honor the Father, the Holy Spirit poured Himself out over Christ's ministry.

The Spirit of Christ is called the Spirit of Truth (John 16:13).

Whenever Jesus speaks, He is speaking the powerful Words of God. His teaching is dynamic because Jesus speaks about vital matters such as the nature of God, the nature of man, relationships, love, sin, judgment, eternity and everlasting life.

Jesus speaks often of the Kingdom of God, Heaven, and even of Hell.

"That was a *Hell* of a sermon, Jesus!" his listeners have marveled.

Jesus' message is also unique because His loving and faithful character is distinctive. The Bible says that the loving character and gracious manner of Christ never changes (Hebrews 13:8).

Thank God we can call on Jesus when we need help speaking.

By faith and prayer, Jesus Himself answers us by giving us power and strength to touch the hearts and souls of other men.

His presence provides the peace and strength we need.

- Jesus' love transforms lives (2 Corinthians 5:17).
- His steadfast love never quits (Lamentations 3:22–23).
- Even when we are faithless, He is faithful (2 Timothy 2:13).

Having a **strong** foundation to build our lives upon is a foundation that we can **greatly lean on** even during the worst storms (Matthew 7:24–26).

Are you willing to trust Jesus to give you the wisdom to lead?

Jesus' Greatest Messages

Jesus spoke two thousand years ago and yet His Words still echo strong into the hearts and souls of millions around the globe.

At times, Jesus' Words are simple enough for a child to grab on to:

"I am the Way, the Truth, and the Life" (John 14:6).
"I am the Bread of Life" (John 6:35).
"I am the Light of the World" (John 8:12).
"I am the Resurrection and the Life" (John 11:25).

In other settings, Jesus' deep discourses went further into the future than anyone ever had before:

The Sermon on the Mount (Matthew 5–7).
Fruitful Discipleship (John 14–16).
(During Jesus' last week on earth.)
Calling out the Pharisees (Matthew 23).
The Mount of Olives Message (Matthew 24–25).
(Jesus speaks about the end of the world.)

Jesus often told stories and parables which illustrated principles about the Kingdom of God.

Parable of the Prodigal Son (Luke 15:11–32).
Parable of the Sower and Seed (Matthew 13:1–9, 18–23).
Parable of the Good Samaritan (Luke 10:30–37).
Parable of the Wheat and the Tares (Matthew 13:24–30).

Which is your favorite sermon or parable from the life of Christ?

More than just great instruction, Jesus delivers His words with love, grace, and kindness. More than just a great speaker, Jesus is a strong leader with great vision.

The compassion of Christ is one of his major characteristics:

Seeing the people, He felt compassion for them, because they were distressed and dispirited like sheep without a shepherd. (Matthew 9:36)

Jesus' Unique Audience and Final Days

Not only is the message of Christ powerful, creative, dynamic, and far above the ordinary, but Jesus also spoke to a unique audience. In some of the most diverse settings of his day, Jesus spoke to the widest sections of society from the poor and blind, to commoners, to religious leaders, to kings and magistrates.

He encouraged the lepers to receive healing (Luke 17:11–19).

He called on Pontius Pilate to know the truth (John 18:36–38).

And to the unruly King Herod, he remained silent (Luke 23:8–12).

At the age of 33, Jesus was confronted by an aggressive group of jealous religious leaders who mocked, whipped, and abused him on show trial. Filled with pride, they rejected Jesus. Their hubris and arrogance has echoed down the ages.

His destiny:

We hereby sentence you, Jesus of Nazareth,
to be led through the streets of the city
carrying your own wooden cross.

To climb up upon a hill called the "Skull,"
and there to be stripped and to be crucified
until dead upon a tree.

For the charges of teaching outside the limits,
loving without fear,
pouring your life out for the oppressed,
the weak, and the lowly.

There you will die outside the city limits
and the boundaries of decency, respect, and gratitude
for simply being who you were all along–
the King who takes away all of our shame.

The sacrificial Lamb who will reign.
God have mercy on us all.

Jesus Comforts the Troubled Hearts

In one of the most unusual public speaking contexts of all time for a leader, Jesus spoke to a group of women carrying His cross on the way to His own execution. Rather than dwell on His own excruciating pain and distress, Jesus stopped long enough to have compassion and show care for these women.

And a great multitude of the people followed Him, and women who also mourned and lamented Him. But Jesus, turning to them, said, "Daughters of Jerusalem, do not weep for Me, but weep for yourselves and for your children. For indeed the days are coming in which they will say, 'Blessed are the barren, wombs that never bore, and breasts which never nursed!' Then they will begin to say to the mountains, 'Fall on us!' and to the hills, 'Cover us!' For if they do these things in the green wood, what will be done in the dry?" (Luke 23:27–31, NKJV)

How fascinating that while most all of His male disciples had fled the scene—except John—those who stayed closest to the cross were the devoted women. Jesus showed care for them, and He also warned them with a prophecy about the coming destruction of Jerusalem, which would follow in the year 70 A.D.

Notice Jesus is also concerned for the children (Luke 23:28).

While suffering to carry a rugged Roman cross, Jesus thought about kids?!

Who does that?

What kind of Shepherd and Savior is this who is mindful of the next generation even when the world has turned against Him?

Jesus cares about the hurting.

Jesus cares about the broken.

Jesus cares about you.

Jesus cares about your soul.

More than just inspiring great speakers and capable leaders, Jesus cares about the condition of our souls. What good is there being a great speaker if our soul is burdened by fear, guilt, wrongdoing, and pride?

More than just helping you to lead well and to speak well, it's the heart of this message that you come to know Jesus in relationship and to follow Him.

If you confess with your mouth Jesus is Lord, and believe in your heart that God raised Him from the dead, you will be saved; for with the heart one believes, resulting in righteousness, and with the mouth he confesses, resulting in salvation. For the Scripture says, "Whoever believes in Him will not be disappointed." (Romans 10:9–11)

More than just joining our Chosen to Speak family, let me encourage you to become a faithful follower of Christ. Out of this relationship comes the love, strength, and the capacity to influence struggling lives around you.

How does one connect with Jesus?

Throw down your own words, passions, and dreams.

Believe upon His Name.

Embrace your own unique calling.

Pick up your cross.

Follow Him.

Pour out your guilt to Him by confessing your sins. Believe upon His Power to forgive you and lead you forward as true King.

Trust Him with your future.

Loving and obeying God brings great joy, despite the cost.

So pause now.

And pray to Jesus. Seek him. He will hear you.

Discovering True Freedom

As we can see from the story of Moses' life, the Power of the Lamb has bought us true freedom to move forward with a bright new start.

By God's Grace and Affection, the Lord receives us to Himself and empowers us to transform the lives around us by His Spirit.

True freedom in Christ is more than just the absence of oppression.

True freedom is more than just the absence of guilt.

Freedom is more than avoidance from pain.

The freedom of Christ is going deep into relationship as we are liberated; to love and to joyfully serve in the Kingdom of God for eternal days.

What joy and what thanksgiving erupted when Moses led the nation out of the bondage and oppression of Egypt.

The four-hundred-year-old dream finally became a reality.

This Hope is born out of just four words from the Lord:

"Let. My. People. Go."

Your Goal Going Forward

With the power of God inside you and the peace of God working through you, the message-of-God-upon-you will bring forth change to your community and delight your Heavenly Father.

Through faith and perseverance in Christ, all things are possible.

Don't put this book on a shelf.

Keep this manuscript near.

Let it roll off your soul.

The Wedding

Down the aisle comes a staggering groom
His heart to be poured out so soon.

With love that pushes him every step
He climbs a hill so that he'll commit
To come to the altar of sacrifice
To pay our debt—sin's great price.

With open arms he's lifted high
To show the world God's love won't die.

His vow is made in costly blood
And is pledged before the angels above
That his grace will last for eternal years
Sealed forever—for the far and near.

Though to him we gave a ring of thorns
He forgets the pain and forgives the scorn.

The veil was lifted in the Holy Place.
The mystery clear—we can see God's face.
His tears of mercy and His eyes that care
Are a glorious portrait of love so rare.

His only kiss came from a spear
And through it all He showed no fear.

Jesus, the groom, gave His all and died.
For the church, his bride, he was crucified.

Jesus loves His church the Bride, and laid His life down for her.
(Ephesians 5:25–27)

Coaching Questions:

I. What positives did you find in this chapter? What challenged you?

II. What do you appreciate most about Jesus as a speaker?

III. What type of teaching of Christ (statement, sermon, or parable) impacts you the most? Why?

IV. Where do you need to align your life more to the Will of God?

V. Where does Jesus acquire His authority? Where have you seen Jesus demonstrate His authority?

VI. What's standing in your way of becoming a follower of Christ?

VII. How can our coaching team pray for you?

Speaking Exercises:

I. Demonstrate an example of speaking from this pathway of discovery:
- Wedding reception speech
- Testimony for church
- Short business presentation
- Short funeral eulogy for a friend
- Or another idea of your own

II. Looking back over this journey, how have you grown as a leader?

III. What new areas do you need to develop next in your speaking?

Next Steps and Feedback

Do you have any feedback from **Chosen to Speak?** How has this story benefitted you as a leader, and what is your takeaway? Leave your input at https://chosentospeak.com/feedback.

Some of you have just read this book to pull away some insights, wisdom or encouragement, and you are content to find the next book. Thanks for jumping on the journey.

Some of you may still need help in the following areas:
- Lacking confidence speaking or awkward speaking
- Struggling to grow as a leader and to find rhythm
- Not fitting into your broken context/community
- Looking for vision for your future direction
- Struggling to gather your team/following

If you connect with any of these statements, you are connecting with us.

Some of you really want **to develop as a leader** and may still be **looking for a coach.** Let us know how you have connected with this story of Moses and start searching out a reliable coach. If you can't locate someone after searching, contact us directly at contact@chosentospeak.com and I'll see if I can help you locate one.

The good Lord may be **calling some of you to be a speaking coach.** Be empowered in the Lord to take this unique book to your team and to your community.

If you want to be a Chosen to Speak Coach, we are longing for capable, discerning leadership to serve the next generation with humility. Contact us directly at contact@chosentospeak.com.

Reasons to become a Coach:
- Relationship with our Chosen to Speak Leadership Team
- Ongoing coaching tips, updates and guidance
- Guiding leaders to find their voice is a unique calling as coaching develops an intimate relationship with clients, and a sacred trust develops as the leader matures.

It takes courage to lead out front. Encouraged people encourage people.
With great encouragement,
Dave Arden
Director, Chosen to Speak

Appendix A

From the context of our Biblical worldview, we define an identity crisis as:

"An internal struggle whereby conflicting forces are pulling an individual in different directions to create physical, emotional, and spiritual strife."

Examples of different types of identity crises include:
- Internal values clash
- Contrasting character qualities
- Relational role conflicts
- Work role conflicts
- Gender role conflicts
- Cultural identity conflicts
- Vision conflicted (and life direction misaligned)
- Life expectations unmet
- Submission conflict (doing God's will vs. our will)

This is not an exhaustive list.

In order to work through inner conflict, a leader benefits from coaching.
- Who am I really?
- Where does my story begin? (family, culture, backstory, history)
- What are my deeper passions?
- How does God view my character struggles?
- How do I discover my calling as a leader?
- How does God view my future?

A deep crisis of identity can be an amazing opportunity for personal growth as we discover our Father's best purposes and plans.

Identity problems create message problems when speaking publicly.

Discover who you are
in relationship to God and in serving Him,
and who you are meant to become.

www.ingramcontent.com/pod-product-compliance
Lightning Source LLC
Chambersburg PA
CBHW062033120526
44592CB00036B/2031